Financial Planning using Excel
Forcasting Planning and Budgeting Techniques

Sue Nugus

ELSEVIER

AMST   NI   SAN F

NDON
O
OKYO

CIMA
PUBLISHING

CIMA Publishing is an imprint of Elsevier
Linacre House, Jordan Hill, Oxford OX2 8DP, UK
30 Corporate Drive, Suite 400, Burlington, MA 01803, USA

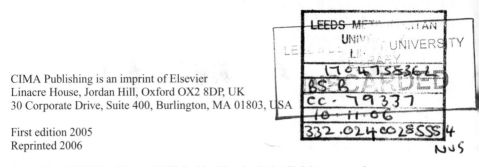

First edition 2005
Reprinted 2006

British Library Cataloguing in Publication Data
A catalogue record for this book is available from the British Library

Library of Congress Cataloging-in-Publication Data
A catalog record for this book is available from the Library of Congress

ISBN–13: 978-0-7506-6355-7
ISBN–10: 0-7506-6355-3

For information on all CIMA publications
visit our website at www.cimapublishing.com

Printed and bound in *Great Britain*

06 07 08 09 10 10 9 8 7 6 5 4 3 2

Working together to grow
libraries in developing countries

www.elsevier.com | www.bookaid.org | www.sabre.org

ELSEVIER   BOOK AID International   Sabre Foundation

Contents

Preface

The objective of this book is to help financial planners improve their spreadsheet skills by providing a structured approach to developing spreadsheets for forecasting, financial planning and budgeting.

The book assumes that the reader is familiar with the basic operation of Excel and is not intended for beginners.

Readers using a different Windows spreadsheet will find that the techniques explained in the book are equally relevant, although it is possible that some command sequences might be slightly different.

The book has been divided into three parts covering the areas of Forecasting, Planning and Budgeting separately. Although it is recommended that readers follow the book from the beginning, the text is also intended as a reference book that will be a valuable aid during model development.

The CD-ROM that accompanies the book contains all the examples described. Instructions for installing and using the CD-ROM are supplied on the CD itself and it is recommended that readers consult the README file contained on the CD.

About the Author

Sue Nugus has been conducting seminars and workshops for accountants and other executives for nearly 20 years. She has worked with the Chartered Institute of Management Accountants and the Institute of Chartered Accountants in England and Wales, and also with the equivalent institutes in Ireland and Scotland.

These seminars and workshops have mostly involved helping accountants and financial managers get the most from their spreadsheets.

The course on which this book is based runs for Management and Chartered Accountants and other executives at least 12 times a year.

In addition to her teaching she has authored and co-authored some 20 books on a wide range of IT subjects that have been published by McGraw-Hill, NCC-Blackwell, and Butterworth-Heinemann.

Sue Nugus also offers consultancy services to those who need assistance in developing advanced spreadsheets.

sue@academic-conferences.org

Part 1

1

Forecasting

I never think of the future; it comes soon enough.

– Boyadjian and Warren, *RISKS, Reading Corporate Signals,* 1987.

Introduction

The objective of a business forecast is to predict or estimate a future activity level such as demand, sales volume, asset requirements, inventory turnover, etc. A forecast is dependent on the analysis of historic and/or current data to produce these estimates. Having accurate forecasts can play an important role in helping an organisation to operate in an efficient and effective manner.

However, before being in a position to create a forecast it is necessary to look carefully at what has happened in the past. As well as examining historic data it is also important to be aware of the organisation's position in its industry and the industry's position in the global marketplace. This is equally true for not-for-profit organisations, which are likely to be more interested in budgeting costs as opposed to profit.

Approaches to forecasting

The process of forecasting can be broadly categorised into two approaches: *objective* or *quantitative* forecasts and *subjective* or *qualitative* forecasts.

Subjective forecasts

Subjective or qualitative forecasts rely to a large extent on an in-depth knowledge of the activity being forecast by those responsible for producing the forecast. The forecast might be created by reading reports and by consulting experts for information and then using this information in a relatively unspecified or unstructured way to predict a required activity. A forecasting method discussed in Chapter 10, called the *composite of individual estimations,* is based on essentially subjective information. The main problem with this approach is that there is no clear methodology which can be analysed to test how a forecast may be improved in order that past mistakes are avoided. As a subjective, or qualitative, forecast is very dependent on the individuals involved, it is prone to problems when the key players responsible for the forecasting process change. This method of forecasting does not usually require much mathematical input and therefore a spreadsheet will play an accompanying role as opposed to a central role.

Objective forecasts

An objective or quantitative approach to forecasting requires a model to be developed which represents the relationships deduced from the observation of one or more different numeric variables. This is generally achieved by first recording historic data and then using these historical facts to hypothesise a relationship between the items to be forecast and the factors believed to be affecting it. The spreadsheet is clearly an ideal tool for this type of analysis and thus can play a central role in the production of such forecasts.

Objective forecasting methods are sometimes considered to be more dependable than subjective methods because they are less affected by what the forecasters would like the result to be. Furthermore, forecasting models can incorporate means of assessing the accuracy of the forecast by comparing what actually happened with what was forecast and adjusting the data to produce more accurate figures in the future. Most of the forecasting examples in the book would be described as objective or quantitative forecasts.

Of course, it is important to appreciate that there has to be an element of subjectivity in all forecasting techniques. At the end of the day what the forecasters know about the business will affect the choice of a particular forecasting technique, and subsequently an in-depth knowledge of the activity being forecast is likely to affect how the forecast data is used to predict activity within the organisation.

Time

Whether a forecast is largely subjective or objective, one of the more common features of a forecast is time, i.e. how far into the future is a forecast designed to look. In this case there can be *short-term* forecasts, *medium-term* forecasts and *long-term* forecasts. The time-span a forecast is considered to fall in will depend on the circumstances and the type of industry involved. In general business terms, short-term forecasts would involve periods of up to one year, medium-term forecasts would consider periods of between one and five years and long-term forecasts would be for longer periods. There are several examples of time-based forecasts in this book, including the *adaptive filtering* model and the *multiplicative time series* model, discussed in Chapter 10.

Forecast units

Whether forecasts are categorised in terms of time or level of objectivity, the forecast unit is also an important variable. For example, a forecast might seek to estimate the level of sales, either as sales units or as sales revenue; or a forecast might seek to establish a level of probability, such as a service level of 99%. It might be appropriate to forecast activity levels such as the numbers of customer service enquiries that are expected between 10 and 11am. In a not-for-profit situation the forecast might be concerned with the expenditure on staff over the forthcoming period.

Finally, any forecast must also be seen in terms of whether it is a one-off estimation or a repetitive calculation. One-off forecasts are normally concerned with large projects and thus may be performed with the aid of considerable financial resources.

A common requirement of those responsible for the budgeting function in an organisation is the need to create ongoing forecasts where there is a need for continuous adjustments to previously forecast figures. These forecasts need to be developed in such a way that actual data can be entered into the model in order that a comparison can be made between the forecast and the actual data. The accuracy of the forecast can then be assessed and adjustments can be made in order to attempt to make the next forecast more accurate.

Forecasting and Excel

As mentioned above, the spreadsheet has a valuable role to play in a range of different forecasting activities, although clearly the objective or quantitative approach particularly lends itself to the numeric analysis tools offered by the spreadsheet. Indeed, in Excel today, as well as the ability to build formulae by referencing data that has been entered into the spreadsheet cells, there are a large number of built-in functions that make the task even easier and open the door to the ability to perform a wider range of analyses.

The problem of course is first discovering just what is available and then learning how to apply the tool to the task in hand. It is hoped that by working through the exercises in this book the reader will be better placed to produce useful Excel-based forecasts.

2

Collecting and Examining the Data

Without systematic measurements, managers have little to guide their actions other than their own experience and judgment. Of course, these will always be important; but as businesses becomes more complex and global in their scope, it becomes increasingly more difficult to rely on intuition alone.

– J. Singleton, E. McLean and E. Altman, *MIS Quarterly*, June 1988.

Data collection

Before selecting a forecasting technique it is necessary to have an appropriate amount of data on which to base the forecast. The quantity and type of data that constitutes 'appropriate' will vary depending on the activity that is to be forecast. At some point, however, historic data will no longer be relevant and it is important for those involved with the forecasting to agree on what constitutes usable data from the outset.

The periodicity of the data is also important. In general terms the input data, i.e. the historic data, should be entered into the spreadsheet using the same periodicity as the output, i.e. the forecast. The main reason for this is that if data is entered into the spreadsheet as monthly figures, for a quarterly forecast, then a degree of calculation is required at this base level. This can lead to an *opportunity for GIGO*.

The acronym GIGO is a long-standing computer term which generally stands for *Garbage In Garbage Out* – implying that if you are not careful with the information you put into a computer you will only get rubbish out. In the spreadsheet environment there can be a slightly different definition, which is, *Garbage In Gospel Out* – because it is not difficult for the spreadsheet to look right, even though the contents may actually be rubbish! I will therefore point out *opportunities for GIGO* throughout the book with accompanying ways of avoiding them.

In the case of the periodicity of data, if the base data or the end result has to be divided by four in order to convert it from monthly to quarterly figures, this requires someone to remember to always do this and to ensure that all updates and amendments that are made to a plan have been adjusted. It is this type of activity that can lead to errors being deeply embedded into spreadsheet systems.

Of course, it is not always possible to have the input and the output data in the same periodicity and if this is the case, it is important to

OPPORTUNITY FOR GIGO

make it clear on the spreadsheet that a change is being made. There is a further discussion on documenting a spreadsheet in Chapter 9.

Examining the data

Once entered into the spreadsheet, the historic data should be examined to ascertain the presence of any obvious patterns. For example, is there evidence of *trend*, *seasonality* or *business cycle*? The quantity of data will affect the types of patterns to be sought. For example, in order to establish the presence of seasonality a sufficient number of periods of data must be available, and business cycles can be considered only by looking at a large number of periods.

First draw a graph

The data shown in the following examples represents historic sales data from which forecasts are to be produced and can be found on the file named RAWDATA.XLS on the CD accompanying the book. The periodicity of the data in each of the examples is monthly, but the number of periods differs in each example. In order to simplify the examination of the data, line graphs have been produced. This is a good example of using simple graphs to look at spreadsheet data which immediately highlights the presence or absence of patterns in the data that would otherwise require mathematical analysis of a set of numbers.

No trend or seasonality

The first data set in Figure 2.1 shows 24 months of historic income values. By looking at the chart it is clear that there is no strong trend, no apparent seasonality and the number of periods is too few to be able to perceive a business cycle. Based on these observations the next period is as likely to increase, decrease or remain the same.

Some evidence of trend

Figure 2.2 shows another set of 24 months of historic income. From the chart it can be seen that looking across the 24 periods the income is increasing, although there are fluctuations in the data. This would indicate an upward trend. Of course, a trend may not

RAWDATA.XLS

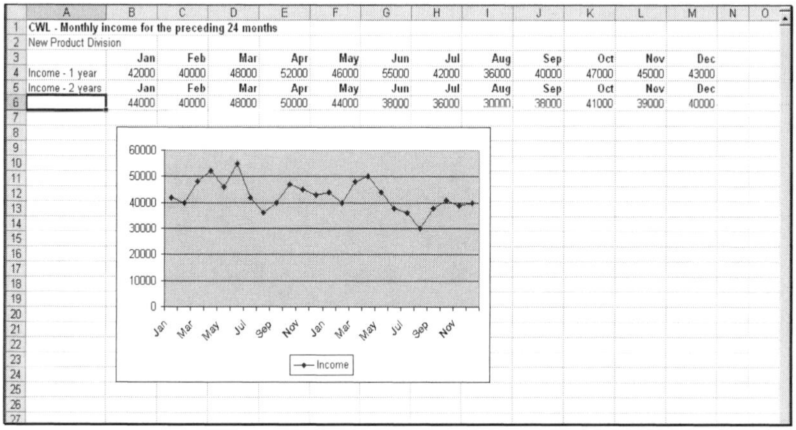

Figure 2.1 Historic data for 24 monthly periods showing no trend

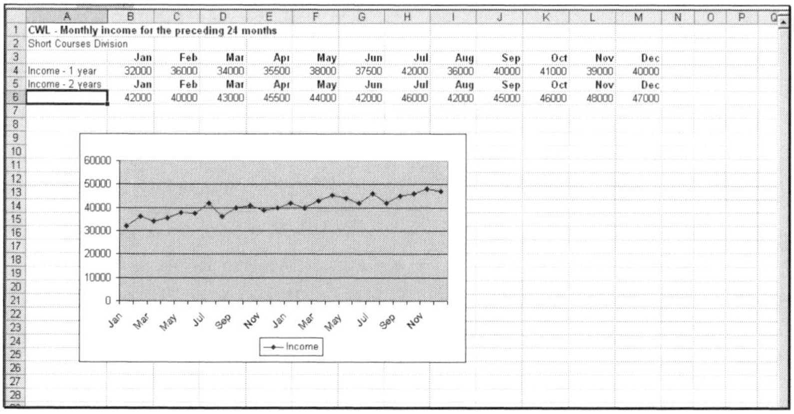

Figure 2.2 Historic data for 24 monthly periods showing some trend

always be favourable and it is important to be able to explain the reason for any trend; for example growth in the market or the success of a marketing plan. On the other hand the data might be representing an increase in costs, causing a downward trend.

Seasonality

Looking at the chart in Figure 2.3, which shows three years of monthly historic income data, in addition to an upward trend, there is a strong indication of seasonality. There appears to be a

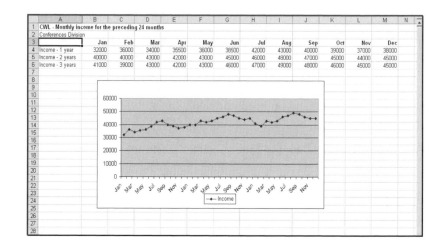

Figure 2.3 Historic data for 24 monthly periods showing evidence of seasonality

similar peak in the data between June and September in all three years, which could indicate a seasonal pattern. To confirm this it is important to refer back to the activity being forecast to ensure that this is indeed the case.

Business cycle

The last set of data to be examined here is shown in Figure 2.4 and consists of quarterly data for the number of conference

	A	B	C	D	E
1	CWL - Quarterly attendance figures for the past 20 years				
2	Conferences Division				
3					
4		QRT 1	QRT 2	QRT 3	QRT 4
5	Now - 1 year	1809	1607	1769	1883
6	Now - 2 years	1823	1705	1799	1695
7	Now - 3 years	1641	1572	1540	1444
8	Now - 4 years	1543	1576	1467	1598
9	Now - 5 years	1485	1485	1485	1485
10	Now - 6 years	1485	1485	1485	1485
11	Now - 7 year	1687	1860	1922	1707
12	Now - 8 years	1868	1634	1771	1797
13	Now - 9 years	1733	1664	1581	1586
14	Now - 10 years	1486	1521	1563	1385
15	Now - 11 years	1500	1605	1706	1726
16	Now - 12 years	1772	1880	1890	1900
17	Now - 13 years	1902	2101	1941	2164
18	Now - 14 years	2215	1904	2249	2165
19	Now - 15 years	2047	1964	1927	1897
20	Now - 16 years	1822	1898	1779	1664
21	Now - 17 years	1631	1656	1892	1850
22	Now - 18 years	1684	1767	1873	1894
23	Now - 19 years	1941	2000	2009	2081
24	Now - 20 years	2076	2234	2033	2203

Figure 2.4 Quarterly data for 20 years indicating a business cycle

participants over the past 20 year period. From the chart it can be seen that there appears to be a five year cyclical pattern to the data. As a business cycle implies a cyclical trend pattern over a longer period of time, the data in this example suggests five yearly peaks and troughs in the number of people that attend conferences, and by looking at the overall business situation at this time this may correspond with periods of growth and recession.

Using statistical measures

Although charts are a useful way of obtaining an overall view of the movement of data, it is also important to be able to describe or summarise the data using statistical measures.

Descriptive statistics

The descriptive statistics included here are the *mean*, the *mode*, the *median*, the *standard deviation*, the *variance* and the *range*.

Figure 2.5 shows the number of emails that are sent each month by day. This is the data from which the descriptive statistics are measured.

DESCRIP.XLS

	A	B	C	D	E	F	G
1	No. emails received by day for each month						
2							
3		Mon	Tues	Wed	Thur	Fri	
4	Jan	570	539	580	563	497	
5	Feb	520	480	510	500	490	
6	Mar	562	588	502	516	540	
7	Apr	568	516	550	562	556	
8	May	555	562	548	548	546	
9	Jun	549	576	560	498	554	
10	Jul	562	553	575	539	531	
11	Aug	586	567	509	529	587	
12	Sep	596	577	574	555	580	
13	Oct	569	550	557	558	563	
14	Nov	562	519	569	530	560	
15	Dec	567	553	524	501	550	
16	Total	6766	6580	6558	6399	6554	

Figure 2.5 Number of emails sent each month by day

The mean, median and mode are described as *measures of central tendency* and offer different ways of presenting a typical or representative value of a data set. The range, the standard deviation and the variance are *measures of dispersion* and refer to the degree to which the observations in a given data set are spread about the arithmetic mean. The mean, often together with the standard deviation, are the most frequently used measures of central tendency. Excel has a series of built-in functions that can be used to produce descriptive statistics.

In the **DESCRIP** worksheet the area B4:F15 has been named DATA. Any rectangular range of cells can be assigned a name in Excel, which has the benefit of offering a description of a range of cells and also can make the referencing of the range easier. To name a range first select the area to be named and then type the chosen name into the Name box, which is located to the left of the edit line at the top of the screen.

Figure 2.6a shows the result of the descriptive statistic functions which can be found on Sheet B of the file **DESCRIP**. In Figure 2.6b the spreadsheet has been set to display the contents on the cells in order that the reader can look at the functions and formulae that have been used. This is achieved by holding down the

CTRL key and then pressing ` key (usually this key also has ¬ and ¦ symbols on it).

	A	B
1	Results of Descriptive Statistics	
2		
3	Number of Observations	100.00
4	Mean	552.30
5	Median	555.00
6	Mode	580.00
7	Minimum	497.00
8	Maximum	599.00
9	Range	102.00
10	Standard Deviation	25.14
11	Variance	631.83
12		

	A	B
2		
3	Number of Observations	=COUNTA(Data)
4	Mean	=AVERAGE(Data)
5	Median	=MEDIAN(Data)
6	Mode	=MODE(Data)
7	Minimum	=MIN(Data)
8	Maximum	=MAX(Data)
9	Range	=ABS(B8-B7)
10	Standard Deviation	=STDEVP(Data)
11	Variance	=VARP(Data)
12		
13		
14		

(a)   (b)

Figure 2.6 Results of descriptive statistics

Number of observations

The number of observations can be counted through the use of the =COUNT function. This function has a number of variations:

=COUNT(. . .)	counts cells containing numbers and numbers entered into the list of arguments.
=COUNTA(. . .)	counts all non-blank cells and numbers entered into the list of arguments.
=COUNTBLANK(. . .)	counts blank cells in the list of arguments.
=COUNTIF(. . .)	counts cells in the list of arguments that satisfy a specified criteria.

Mean

The *mean* or *arithmetic mean* is defined as follows:

$$\text{sample mean} = \frac{\text{total of a number of sample values}}{\text{the number of sample values}}$$

To calculate the sample arithmetic mean of the production weights the AVERAGE function is used as follows in cell B4.

=AVERAGE(DATA)

It is important to note that the AVERAGE function totals the cells containing values and divides by the number of cells that contain values. In certain situations this may not produce the required results and it might be necessary to ensure that zero has been entered into blank cells in order that the function sees the cell as containing a value.

OPPORTUNITY FOR GIGO

Sample median

The *sample median* is defined as the middle value when the data values are ranked in increasing, or decreasing, order of magnitude. The following formula in cell B5 uses the MEDIAN function to calculate the median value for the production weights:

=MEDIAN(DATA)

Sample mode

The sample mode is defined as the value in an argument which occurs most frequently. The following is required to calculate the mode of the production weights.

=MODE(DATA)

The mode may not be unique, as there can be multiple values that return an equal, but most frequently occurring value. In this case the mode function returns the first value in the argument that occurs most frequently. Furthermore, if every value in the sample data set is different, there is no mode and the function will return an N/A result.

Minimum and maximum

It is often useful to know the smallest and the largest value in a data series and the MINIMUM and MAXIMUM functions have been used in cells B7 and B8 to calculate this as follows:

=MIN(DATA)

=MAX(DATA)

TECHNIQUE
TIP!

By including a value within the argument for the MIN and MAX functions it is possible to ensure that the value in a cell is within specified boundaries. For example, to return the lowest value in a range, but to ensure that the result was never higher than 500, the following could be used:

=MIN(B4:B16, 500)

In this instance the system will look at the values in the range B4:B16 and will also look at the value 500 and if 500 is the lowest value in the range this will be the result.

The range

The range is defined as the difference between the largest and smallest values in a data series. The following formula can be used to calculate the range of the number of emails sent by referencing the already calculated minimum and maximum values:

=B8–B7

Sample standard deviation

The sample standard deviation s is obtained by summing the squares of the differences between each value and the sample mean, dividing by $n - 1$, and then taking the square root. Therefore the algebraic formula for the sample standard deviation is:

$$s = \sqrt{\frac{\Sigma x^2 - \frac{(\Sigma x)^2}{n}}{n - 1}}$$

In other words the standard deviation is the square root of the variance of all individual values from the mean. The more variation in the data, the higher the standard deviation will be. If there is no variation at all, the standard deviation will be zero. It can never be negative.

To calculate the standard deviation for the number of emails sent the following can be entered into cell B10:

=STDEV(DATA)

Note that this function assumes a sample population. If the data represents the entire population then STDEVP() should be used.

Sample variance

The sample variance is the square of the standard deviation. The formula required to calculate the sample variance of the number of emails sent in cell B11 is:

=VAR(DATA)

In the same way as the standard deviation, the above function assumes that sample data is being used. For the entire population, the function VARP() is required.

Data Analysis Command

A quick way of producing a set of descriptive statistics on a range of data is to use the TOOLS : DATA ANALYSIS : DESCRIPTIVE STATISTICS command. Figure 2.7 shows the result of this on the number of emails sent during January.

	A	B	C	D	E	F
17	Descriptive Statistics on the number of emails sent in January					
18						
19		Jan				
20						
21		Mean	549.8			
22		Standard Error	14.830374			
23		Median	563			
24		Mode	#N/A			
25		Standard Deviation	33.161725			
26		Sample Variance	1099.7			
27		Kurtosis	1.1106815			
28		Skewness	-1.261058			
29		Range	83			
30		Minimum	497			
31		Maximum	580			
32		Sum	2749			
33		Count	5			
34						
35						

Figure 2.7 Results of descriptive statistics command

In addition to the statistics already described this command provides the standard error, the kurtosis and the skewness.

The standard error of a sample of sample size n is the sample's standard deviation divided by $\sqrt{n}$. It therefore estimates the standard deviation of the sample mean based on the population mean (Press et al. 1992, p. 465)[1].

The kurtosis can be defined as the degree of peakedness of a distribution.

Skewness is a measure of the degree of asymmetry of a distribution. If the left tail (tail at small end of the distribution) is more pronounced that the right tail (tail at the large end of the distribution), the function is said to have negative skewness. If the reverse is true, it has positive skew.[2]

---

[1] Press, W.H.; Flannery, B.P.; Teukolsky, S.A.; and Vetterling, W.T. *Numerical Recipes in FORTRAN: The Art of Scientific Computing, 2nd ed.* Cambridge, England: Cambridge University Press, 1992.

[2] http://www.mathworld.com

Summary

The first step in preparing any forecasting system is to carefully examine the available data in order to ascertain the presence of a trend, a seasonal pattern or a business cycle. Simply looking as the data, or eyeballing it as it is sometimes described, can be good enough for this purpose. It is then useful to prepare a set of descriptive statistics such as those described in this chapter in order to further understand the situation described by the data. These statistics may be used as a first step in embarking on an appropriate forecasting technique.

3

Smoothing Techniques

Good judgment is usually the result of experience. And experience is frequently the result of bad judgment.

— R.E. Neustadt and E.R. May, *Thinking in Time*, 1986.

Introduction

Smoothing refers to looking at the underlying pattern of a set of data to establish an estimate of future values. Smoothing can be achieved through a range of different techniques, including the use of the AVERAGE function and the exponential smoothing formula. To be able to use any smoothing technique a series of historic data is required.

Estimating a single value for the next period is called *univariate analysis* and there are a number of techniques that can be used to produce the forecast value. These include:

◆ estimation of the value
◆ using the last known value
◆ calculating the average or arithmetic mean of the historic data.

Estimation of the value is a subjective approach that depends entirely on the forecaster knowing the activity being forecast and being able to judge the outcome for the next period. In some cases this is referred to as *guesstimation*.

In a situation where the examination of the historic data has shown no evidence of a trend then using the last known value can be an appropriate method of estimation.

Using an average or arithmetic mean produces a value that is typical or representative of a given set of data. The algebraic formula for the arithmetic mean is:

$$F_t = (1/N)\Sigma X_t$$

where F_t = the forecast, N = number of observations and X_t = historic observations. The arithmetic mean or the simple average of a data set produces a straight line through the data. Although this is not especially useful as a forecasting tool, having the mean of a series of historic values is important for comparison purposes.

Figure 3.1 takes the first set of data examined in Chapter 2 and gives examples of an estimation, the last observation and the arithmetic mean or average.

SMOOTH.XLS

The AVERAGE function has been used to calculate the arithmetic mean.

All three of the techniques shown in Figure 3.1 are regularly used in situations where there is little or no trend to influence the selection of a different forecasting approach.

The graph in Figure 3.1 shows the arithmetic mean plotted against the historic data. From this it can be seen that the arithmetic mean of 42,666 is a measure of central tendency, and there are approximately as many data points above as there are below the line.

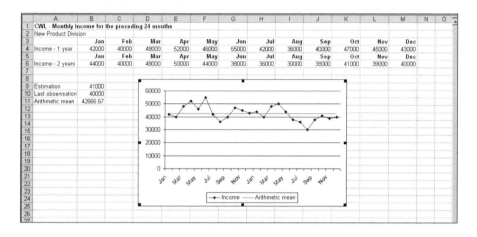

Figure 3.1 Examples of an estimation, last observation and arithmetic mean

Moving averages

In an environment in which the data does not exhibit any significant trend and when using an average to calculate a future expected value, the earlier historic observations may have less relevance than the more recent observations, especially in cases where there is little evidence of trend or seasonality. In this case a *moving average* can be employed which allows early values to be dropped as later values are added. The algebraic formula for a moving average is as follows:

$$F_t = (1/N)\Sigma X_{t-i}$$

where F_t = the forecast, N = number of observations, X_t = historic observations and i = change in X_t variables.

The greater the value of N, the less the forecast will be affected by random fluctuations, or the greater the degree of *smoothing*. Furthermore, the greater the number of observations the slower the forecast is to respond to changes in the underlying pattern of the data. Figure 3.2 illustrates a three month moving average and a five month moving average.

	A	B	C	D	E	F	G	H	I	J	K	L	M
1	CWL - Monthly income for the preceding 24 months												
2	Short Courses Division												
3		Jan	Feb	Mar	Apr	May	Jun	Jul	Aug	Sep	Oct	Nov	Dec
4	Income - 1 year	32000	36000	34000	35500	38000	37500	42000	36000	40000	41000	39000	40000
5													
6	3 month moving avg			34000	35166.7	35833.33	37000.00	39166.67	38500.00	39333.33	39000.00	40000.00	40000.00
7	5 month moving avg					35100.00	36200.00	37400.00	37800.00	38700.00	39300.00	39600.00	39200.00

Figure 3.2 Three and five month moving averages

The three month moving average shown by the green line in Figure 3.2 reflects changes in the data and is easily influenced by irregularities and fluctuations. The five month moving average shown by the blue line, on the other hand, is smoother and shows less influence of irregularities and fluctuations.

The formula in cell D6 is =AVERAGE(B4:D4). This formula has then been extrapolated through to M6.

Weighted moving average

In addition to restricting the number of historic observations that are incorporated into a moving average, it is sometimes necessary to place more emphasis on some data points than on others. To this end a *weighted moving average* technique can be applied to the data. There are a number of different approaches to using weighted moving averages and the *proportional* and *trend adjusted* methods are discussed here.

Proportional method

With the proportional method each value in the moving average is multiplied by a specified weight, and the total of the weights usually equals 1. The algebraic formula for this method is as follows:

$$F_t = P_1X_1 + P_2X_2 + \cdots + P_nX_n$$

where F_t = the forecast, X_t = historic observations and

$$P_1 + P_2 + \cdots + P_{n_1} = 1$$

Figure 3.3 shows the results of using the proportional method for calculating a three month weighted moving average which can then be compared to the previously calculated three month moving average without weights.

	A	B	C	D	E	F	G	H	I	J	K	L	M
1	CWL - Monthly income for the preceding 24 months												
2	Short Courses Division												
3		Jan	Feb	Mar	Apr	May	Jun	Jul	Aug	Sep	Oct	Nov	Dec
4	Income - 1 year	32000	36000	34000	35500	38000	37500	42000	36000	40000	41000	39000	40000
5													
6	3 month moving avg			34000	35166.7	35833.33	37000.00	39166.67	38500.00	39333.33	39000.00	40000.00	40000.00
7	3 month weighted moving average			34200	35150	36450	37250	39850	38100	39200	39700	39800	39900
8													
9	Proportional weights	0.2	0.3	0.5									

Figure 3.3 Three month moving average using the proportional method

The effect of the weights that have been used in the above example is to place a greater emphasis on the most recent historical observation. In other words the most recent occurrence is most important when determining the next occurrence. By looking at the actual value for the forecast period the weights could be changed in an attempt to produce a more accurate forecast for the next period.

Figure 3.4 shows the formula required for the weighted moving average and Figure 3.5 shows the unweighted and weighted moving averages plotted together on the same graph.

TECHNIQUE
TIP!

Note that the cell references to the proportional weights are absolute, i.e. $B$9, $C$9 and $D$9. This means that when the formula is

	A	B	C	D	E
1	**CWL - Monthly income for the preceding 24 months**				
2	Short Courses Division				
3		Jan	Feb	Mar	Apr
4	Income - 1 year	32000	36000	34000	35500
5					
6	3 month moving avg			=AVERAGE(B4:D4)	=AVERAGE(C4:E4)
7	3 month weighted moving average			=B4*$B$9+C4*$C$9	=C4*$B$9+D4*$C$9
8					
9	Proportional weights	0.2	0.3	0.5	
10					

Figure 3.4 Formulae required for weighted moving average

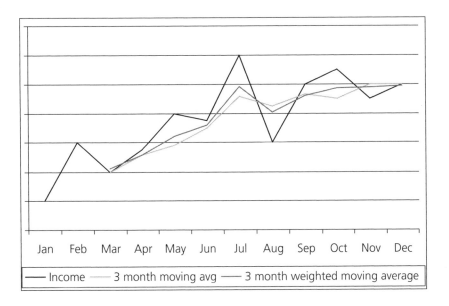

Figure 3.5 Chart showing unweighted and weighted three month moving average

copied the reference to cells B9, C9 and D9 remain fixed, whilst the other cell references are relative.

Trend adjusted method

If, as a result of examining the data, there is evidence of a trend, then a *trend adjusted* method of weighting the average can be applied. This involves assigning greater weights to more recent observations. There are a number of approaches to applying trend adjusted weights and the following is an example:

$$F_t = 2X_{t-1} - X_{t-2}$$

In this example the last observation is doubled before the observation before that is subtracted. This has the effect of using twice the increase in the value of the observations from period $t-2$ to $t-1$ in the forecast.

The effect of using this technique on the second set of data from Chapter 2 which showed some evidence of trend can be seen in Figure 3.6, and Figure 3.7 shows the results graphically.

	A	B	C	D	E	F	G	H	I	J	K	L	M	N
1	CWL - Monthly income for the preceding 24 months													
2	Conferences Division													
3			Jan	Feb	Mar	Apr	May	Jun	Jul	Aug	Sep	Oct	Nov	Dec
4	Income - 1 year		32000	36000	34000	35500	36000	38500	42000	43000	40000	41500	42200	44000
5														
6	Trend adjusted moving average			40000	32000	37000	36500	41000	45500	44000	37000	43000	42900	45800
7														

Figure 3.6 Trend adjusted moving average

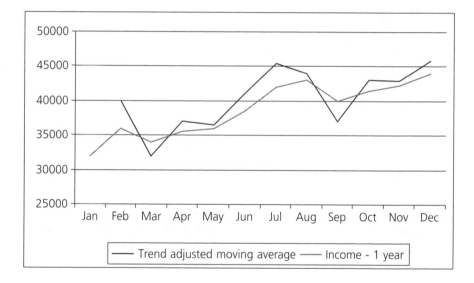

Figure 3.7 Trend adjusted moving average chart

The formula required in cell C5, which can be extrapolated for the remaining periods, is:

=(C3*2)−B3

Adaptive filtering

Adaptive filtering is a technique used to re-evaluate the individual weights in a weighted average model to take into account the experience of actual results. Thus adaptive filtering allows a weighted average technique to learn from past errors and provides a systematic approach to adjusting the weights to the latest information available. The algebraic formula for adaptive filtering is as follows:

$$W'_t = W_t + 2K[(X_t - F_t)/X^2]X_{t-1}$$

where W'_t = the updated weight, W_t = the previous weight, X_t = the observation at time t, K = a constant, i.e. the training constant which may not be greater than $1/n$, and X = the largest of the most recent n values of X_t. Figure 3.8 is a model for adaptive filtering.

	A	B	C	D	E	F
1	Weighted Moving Average with adaptive filtering					
2						
3			Historic quarterly sales data			
4	QUARTER	1	2	3	4	
5	ACTUAL SALES	12567	13456	9504	11000	
6	OPEN WEIGHTS	0.20	0.20	0.20	0.40	
7						
8			FORECAST FOR 20XX			
9	QUARTER	5	6	7	8	
10	FORECAST	11505	11789	0	0	
11	ACTUAL SALES	11670	0	0		
12						
13	ADAPTIVE FILTERING - RECALCULATION OF NEW WEIGHTS					
14						
15	Adjusted weights for Qrt 6 forecast	0.21	0.21	0.21	0.41	
16	Adjusted weights for Qrt 7 forecast	0.00	0.00	0.00	0.00	
17	Adjusted weights for Qrt 8 forecast	0.00	0.00	0.00	0.00	
18						
19						

Figure 3.8 Model for adaptive filtering

The plan consists of a set of historic quarterly sales figures and cell B10 is the initial forecast for the first quarter of 1997 which is calculated by multiplying the historic quarterly data by the opening proportional weights in row 6. Thus the formula for cell B10 is:

=B5*B6+C5*C6+D5*D6+E5*E6

When the actual sales for the first quarter become available the value is entered into cell B11. The adaptive filtering formula in cell B15, which is extrapolated into cells C15 through E15, calculates revised weights which are then referenced in cell C10 when the forecast for the second quarter is calculated. The following is the formula entered into cell B15 and copied across to cell E15.

$$=B6+2*0.25*(($B$11-$B$10)/$B$5^2)*B5$$

The forecast formula for the second quarter of 1997 in cell C10 is therefore:

$$=C5*B15+D5*C15+E5*D15+B11*E15$$

It is not possible to copy the above formula as the references to the previous quarters are not in the same row and the revised weights for each quarter are also on different rows.

The adjusted weights will no longer total 1 because if the actual amount is less than the forecast then the combined weights will end up being less than 1. The converse is true in that if the actual amount is more than the forecast, the combined weights will total more than 1.

In order to test the accuracy of the system, enter an actual value that exactly matches the forecast. In this case the weights should not change, as no adjustment is required.

TECHNIQUE
TIP!

Exponential smoothing

Exponential smoothing is a weighted moving average technique which is especially effective when frequent re-forecasting is required, and when the forecasts must be achieved quickly. It is a short-term forecasting technique that is frequently used in the production and inventory environment, where only the next period's value is required to be forecast. Because only three numbers are required to perform exponential smoothing, this technique is simple to update. The data required are the historic observation, the latest data observation and the smoothing coefficient, or constant.

The smoothing coefficient α is a value between 0 and 1. A small value of, say, between 0.05 and 0.10 results in a high degree of smoothing and has the same effect as a large number of observations in a moving average calculation. A high coefficient value results in less smoothing and thus a high responsiveness to variations in the data. In the extreme, if the coefficient is zero then the next period's forecast will be the same as the last period's forecast and if the coefficient is one, or unity, then the next period's forecast will be the same as the current period's data.

The primary assumption used in the simple form of this smoothing technique is that the data is stationary, i.e. that there is a clear trend present. Advanced exponential smoothing techniques are required if a trend or cycle is present in the data.

The algebraic formula for simple exponential smoothing is:

$$F_t = X_t + (1 - \alpha)F_{t-1}$$

where F_{t-1} = the previous forecast, X_t = the current observation and α = the smoothing coefficient. Figure 3.9 shows an example of exponential smoothing.

	A	B	C	D	E	F	G	H	I	J	K	L	M	N
1	Simple Exponential Smoothing													
2														
3	Historic monthly income data													
4			JAN	FEB	MAR	APR	MAY	JUN	JUL	AUG	SEP	OCT	NOV	DEC
5	Income - 1 year	114	121	119	120	115	125	119	120	128	119	122	118	
6	E-S Coefficient	0.4												
7	Forecast	114	117	118	119	117	120	120	120	123	121	122	120	
8														

Figure 3.9 Forecast using the exponential smoothing technique

The smoothing coefficient is first used in the second period of the forecast and so in Figure 3.9 the formula for cell C6 is:

=C4*$B$5+(1−$B$5)*B6

With a low coefficient value of 0.20 a high degree of smoothing is expected and this is shown in the graph in Figure 3.10. Figure 3.11 shows the effect of a high smoothing coefficient where 0.80 has been entered into cell B5.

As exponential smoothing does not require a great deal of historic data, it is another useful tool for short-term forecasts.

The spreadsheet examples used in this chapter do not require the use of complicated spreadsheet functions and formulae. Indeed the AVERAGE function has been the main tool. However, the chapter

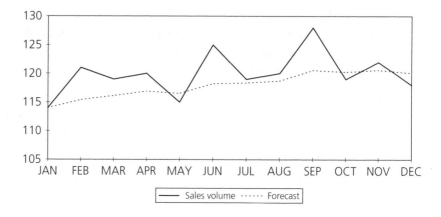

Figure 3.10 Forecast with a low coefficient of 0.20

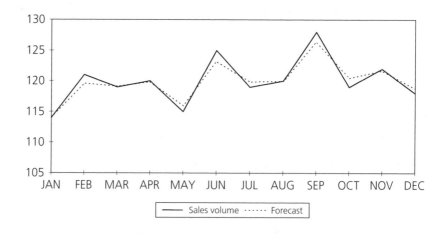

Figure 3.11 Forecast with a high coefficient of 0.80

has illustrated that having ascertained the algebraic formula for a particular technique it is not difficult to translate this into a formula that the spreadsheet understands. Once the formulae have been entered and tested the models can be used again and again with different data.

As with any forecasting technique it is important to always check what actually happened with the activity that was being forecast in order to ascertain how accurate the forecast was, and where necessary be able to adjust the forecast to better reflect the situation next time.

Summary

There are many different approaches to averaging and smoothing as a means of forecasting. Moving averages and weighted moving averages are useful as a first step, especially when there is no clear evidence of trend, seasonality or cycles. Adaptive filtering is very useful in a continuous forecasting situation where the actual data is available to assist in forecasting the next period.

4

Regression Analysis

"One can't believe impossible things," said Alice. "I dare say you haven't had much practice," said the Queen. "When I was your age, I always did it for half-an-hour a day. Why, sometimes I've believed as many as six impossible things before breakfast."

– Lewis Carroll, *Through the Looking Glass*, 1982.

Introduction

Many forecasting methods are based on the assumption that the variable being forecast is related to something else. Thus sales might vary according to the amount spent on advertising, or the life of a component might be determined by how long it has been held in the warehouse. Regression analysis is a widely used tool for analysing the relationship between such variables and using these variables for prediction purposes. For example, can variations in the number of marketing emails sent each month be used to help predict the income to the conference business?

To answer this question the first step is to establish whether there is indeed a relationship between the number of marketing emails sent and the income. This is achieved by recording the required information over a period of time and then plotting the data on a *scatter diagram*.

Figure 4.1 shows a set of data collected monthly for a period of one year.

REGRESSION.XLS

	A	B	C	D
1	CWL Emails sent monthly vs income			
2	Month	No. emails	Income	
3	Jan	96	15000	
4	Feb	106	15670	
5	Mar	198	25300	
6	Apr	195	21100	
7	May	135	18600	
8	Jun	44	12000	
9	Jul	120	17230	
10	Aug	171	20700	
11	Sep	180	20990	
12	Oct	50	12400	
13	Nov	75	13100	
14	Dec	21	10200	
15	Total	**1391**	**202290**	

Figure 4.1 Monthly income and number of emails sent

Before drawing a scatter diagram from the data it should be sorted by the number of emails sent. This is achieved by first selecting the range A2:C14 and then using the Data Sort command to sort on column B in ascending order (Figure 4.2).

	A	B	C	D
1	CWL Emails sent monthly vs income			
2	Month	No. emails	Income	
3	Dec	21	10200	
4	Jun	44	12000	
5	Oct	50	12400	
6	Nov	75	13100	
7	Jan	96	15000	
8	Feb	106	15670	
9	Jul	120	17230	
10	May	135	18600	
11	Aug	171	20700	
12	Sep	180	20990	
13	Apr	195	21100	
14	Mar	198	25300	
15	Total	**1391**	**202290**	

Figure 4.2 Data sorted by number of emails sent

A scatter diagram is produced by selecting the range B3:C14, clicking on the Graph icon on the toolbar and selecting XY-scatter. From the sub-choices of XY-graphs take the option with no lines. Figure 4.3 is the resulting chart.

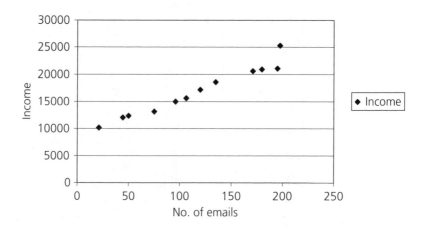

Figure 4.3 Scatter diagram showing relationship between the number of emails sent and the monthly income

By looking at the chart in Figure 4.3 it is clear that there is a strong linear relationship between the two variables. Had this not been the case the points on the graph would be scattered more widely. Figure 4.4 is scatter diagram showing the number of aircraft sold at different rainfall levels and it is clear from this graph that there is no relationship between these two variables, as one would of course expect.

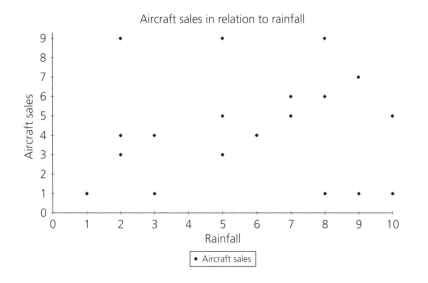

Figure 4.4 Scatter diagram showing no discernible relationship between the variables

Having established a linear relationship between the two variables it is useful to fit a *least square line* to the data, and this is referred to as *simple linear regression*[1]. Simple here implies that only one variable is being used to predict another as opposed to *multiple linear regression* which is discussed later in this chapter.

The algebraic formula for fitting a straight line is:

$$Y = MX + c$$

where Y = the dependent variable, M = the slope or gradient of the line (and is sometimes called the regression coefficient), X = the

---

[1] The word 'regression' originates from the nineteenth century when Galton collected the heights of fathers and their sons and put forward the idea that since very tall fathers tended to have slightly shorter sons and very short fathers tended to have slightly taller sons, there would be what he termed a 'regression to the mean' (D. Rees, 1991, *Essential Statistics*, Chapman and Hall).

independent variable and c is the constant, or intercept, sometimes referred to as the Y intercept. The c is the value of Y when X is zero. It is the base value of Y before any increase or decrease in X is taken into account. The dependent variable (Y) is the variable to be predicted which in the above example would be the income, and the independent variable (X) is the variable used to do the predicting, which in this case refers to the number of emails sent.

In defining the least square line consider the annotated graph in Figure 4.5. For any given value of X there is a difference between $Y1$ and the value of Y determined by the line. The difference is denoted by D, which is referred to as a *deviation*, *residual* or *error*. The least square line is defined as the line through a data set that has the property of minimising the sum of any given set of D^2s.

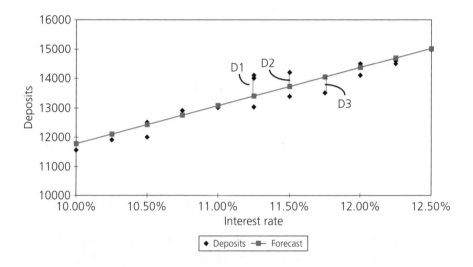

Figure 4.5 Least square line

Given that the least square line approximation has the form $Y = MX + c$ this formula can be broken down as follows:

$$m = \frac{N\Sigma XY - (\Sigma X)(\Sigma Y)}{N\Sigma X^2 - (\Sigma X)^2}$$

and

$$c = \frac{(\Sigma Y)(\Sigma X)^2 - (\Sigma X)(\Sigma XY)}{N\Sigma X^2 - (\Sigma X)^2}$$

where N = the number of data points available, X = the sum of the X data points, Y = the sum of the Y data points and XY = the sum of the product of each set of data.

Having established the equation representing the least square line, an estimate of a value for Y corresponding to a value for X may be obtained. When the least square line is being used in this way it has a *regression line* of Y on X, since Y is estimated from a value of X.

Calculating the least square line

The least square line can be calculated either through the use of the FORECAST function or the TOOLS DATA ANALYSIS REGRESSION command.

The function approach

Figure 4.6 shows the results of the Excel FORECAST function. The following formula was entered into cell D5.

=FORECAST(A5,$B$5:$B$23,$A$5:$A$23)

	A	B	C	D
1	Regression Analysis using Standard Formulae.			
2	INTEREST RATES AND CASH DEPOSITS			
3	(Independent - X)	(Dependent - Y)		
4	Interest rates	Deposits		Forecast
5	10.00%	11550		11768.09
6	10.25%	11900		12093.55
7	10.50%	12500		12419.00
8	10.50%	11990		12419.00
9	10.75%	12900		12744.45
10	11.00%	13000		13069.91
11	11.25%	14000		13395.36
12	11.25%	13020		13395.36
13	11.25%	14000		13395.36
14	11.25%	14100		13395.36
15	11.50%	13380		13720.81
16	11.50%	14200		13720.81
17	11.75%	13500		14046.27
18	11.75%	14050		14046.27
19	12.00%	14500		14371.72
20	12.00%	14100		14371.72
21	12.25%	14500		14697.17
22	12.25%	14600		14697.17
23	12.50%	15000		15022.62

Figure 4.6 Calculated straight line using the Excel FORECAST function

Note that in the above formula it is important to reference the range for the dependent variable first, followed by the range for the independent variable. These references are absolute in order that they remain fixed when the formula is extrapolated for the remaining cells in the range.

The data in column E can now be plotted as a line onto the scatter diagram. A simple way to do this in Excel is to select the range, Copy it to the Clipboard, access and select the chart and then select Paste. Figure 4.7 shows the forecast line on the scatter diagram.

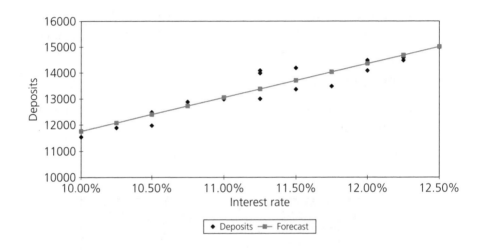

Figure 4.7 Scatter diagram with regression line

The regression line and regression equation applies only within the range of the independent or X range of data. The line should not be extrapolated much below the minimum value of X or above the maximum value of X. Similarly the regression equation should not be used for values of X outside the range of data.

Two other Excel functions that are useful in this context are INTERCEPT and SLOPE which calculate the values for c and M respectively in the formula $Y = MX + c$. Figure 4.8 shows the results of these functions. The following formulae were entered into cells E5 and F5 respectively:

```
=INTERCEPT(B5:B23,A5:A23)
=SLOPE(B5:B23,A5:A23)
```

	A	B	C	D	E	F	G
2	INTEREST RATES AND CASH DEPOSITS						
3	(Independent - X)	(Dependent - Y)					
4	Interest rates	Deposits		Forecast	Intercept	Slope	Forecast
5	10.00%	11550		11768.09	-1250.02	130181.2	11768.09
6	10.25%	11900		12093.55			
7	10.50%	12500		12419.00			
8	10.50%	11990		12419.00			
9	10.75%	12900		12744.45			
10	11.00%	13000		13069.91			
11	11.25%	14000		13395.36			
12	11.25%	13020		13395.36			
13	11.25%	14000		13395.36			
14	11.25%	14100		13395.36			
15	11.50%	13380		13720.81			
16	11.50%	14200		13720.81			
17	11.75%	13500		14046.27			
18	11.75%	14050		14046.27			
19	12.00%	14500		14371.72			
20	12.00%	14100		14371.72			
21	12.25%	14500		14697.17			
22	12.25%	14600		14697.17			
23	12.50%	15000		15022.62			

Figure 4.8 Results of Excel INTERCEPT and SLOPE functions

The results of these two functions can be used to calculate the forecast which is useful as an auditing tool to cross-check the result produced using the FORECAST function. The following formula is required in cell G5:

=$F$5*A5+$E$5

The Command Approach

To use the Regression command in Excel it is necessary to have the Analysis Toolpak[2] installed and enabled. Once enabled Data Analysis becomes the last option on the Tools menu and within Data Analysis one of the options is Regression. The command requires references to the X and Y data and a location for the output. Figure 4.9 shows the results of the command where the output range was selected as a new worksheet.

---

[2] The Analysis Toolpak is a standard part of the Excel package, but if a custom installation was selected during setup it is possible that this option was not selected. Refer to your Excel manual for further information on installation.

	A	B	C	D	E	F	G	H	I
1	SUMMARY OUTPUT								
2									
3	Regression Statistics								
4	Multiple R	0.93							
5	R Square	0.86							
6	Adjusted R Square	0.86							
7	Standard Error	380.14							
8	Observations	19.00							
9									
10	ANOVA								
11		df	SS	MS	F	Significance F			
12	Regression	1.00	15508858.98	15508858.98	107.32	0.00			
13	Residual	17.00	2456614.70	144506.75					
14	Total	18.00	17965473.68						
15									
16		Coefficients	Standard Error	t Stat	P-value	Lower 95%	Upper 95%	Lower 95.0%	Upper 95.0%
17	Intercept	-1250.02	1427.93	-0.88	0.39	-4262.70	1762.66	-4262.70	1762.66
18	Interest rates	130181.16	12566.15	10.36	0.00	103668.87	156693.46	103668.87	156693.46
19									

Figure 4.9 Results of Regression command

The regression formula can be created by referencing the intercept or constant in cell B17 and the X coefficient in cell B18.

Function vs command

The previous section has explained how to perform regression analysis using spreadsheet functions and spreadsheet commands. It is generally preferable to apply functions as opposed to commands wherever possible. This is because functions are dynamic formulae that are recalculated when anything in the spreadsheet changes. Therefore having set up a model such as the one used in this chapter, a different set of sample data could be entered into columns A and B and all the regression formulae and the chart will automatically reflect the changed data. This is not the case with a command, because on executing the command only the resulting values are placed in the spreadsheet without the underlying formula. Therefore to recalculate after making a change it is necessary to execute the Regression command again.

The graphic approach

Excel has the ability to plot a trendline onto a chart without having to calculate the equation beforehand. Figure 4.10 shows the original scatter diagram on which the data series has been selected and the command Insert Trendline has been taken.

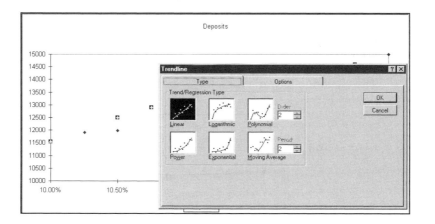

Figure 4.10 Inserting a trendline onto an Excel chart

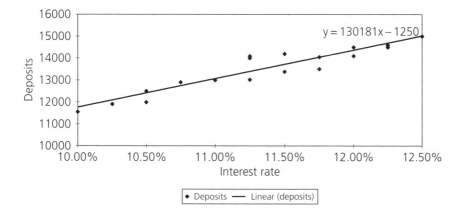

$$y = 130181x - 1250$$

Figure 4.11 Trendline inserted onto an Excel chart

The first option is most suitable for this example, but non-linear trendlines can also be inserted if appropriate. Figure 4.11 shows the resulting trendline. Although the individual calculations behind the line cannot be seen, selecting FORMAT TRENDLINE OPTIONS allows the formula to be displayed as shown in Figure 4.11.

Standard error

An additional refinement of linear regression is to incorporate the *standard error* of the estimate. The standard error has many of the properties analogous to the standard deviation.

For example, if lines are drawn on either side of the regression line of Y on X at respective vertical distances, confidence limits may be established.

The algebraic formula for a 95% confidence limit is:

$$(a + bx_0) \pm ts_r\sqrt{\left[\frac{1}{n} + \frac{(x_0 - \bar{x})^2}{\sum x^2 - \dfrac{(\sum x)^2}{n}}\right]}$$

Figure 4.12 shows the results of calculating upper and lower confidence limits. Two columns have been inserted into the original spreadsheet so that the already calculated forecast is in column E and the lower and upper standard errors will be placed in columns C and D respectively. The formula required in cell C5 to calculate the lower confidence limit is as follows.

=E5−'LR COMMAND'!$D$18*'LR COMMAND'!$B$7*SQRT
   (1+1/'LR COMMAND'!$B$8+(A5−AVERAGE($A$5:$A$23)^2/
   'LR COMMAND'!$B$8*STDEV($A$5:$A$23)))

	A	B	C	D	E
1	Regression Analysis using Standard Formulae.				
2	INTEREST RATES AND CASH DEPOSITS				
3	(Independent - X)	(Dependent - Y)	Standard error		
4	Interest rates	Deposits	Lower limit	Upper limit	Forecast
5	10.00%	11550	7540.10	15996.09	11768.09
6	10.25%	11900	7860.97	16326.12	12093.55
7	10.50%	12500	8181.85	16656.15	12419.00
8	10.50%	11990	8181.85	16656.15	12419.00
9	10.75%	12900	8502.73	16986.18	12744.45
10	11.00%	13000	8823.61	17316.20	13069.91
11	11.25%	14000	9144.50	17646.22	13395.36
12	11.25%	13020	9144.50	17646.22	13395.36
13	11.25%	14000	9144.50	17646.22	13395.36
14	11.25%	14100	9144.50	17646.22	13395.36
15	11.50%	13380	9465.40	17976.23	13720.81
16	11.50%	14200	9465.40	17976.23	13720.81
17	11.75%	13500	9786.30	18306.23	14046.27
18	11.75%	14050	9786.30	18306.23	14046.27
19	12.00%	14500	10107.20	18636.23	14371.72
20	12.00%	14100	10107.20	18636.23	14371.72
21	12.25%	14500	10428.11	18966.23	14697.17
22	12.25%	14600	10428.11	18966.23	14697.17
23	12.50%	15000	10749.03	19296.22	15022.62

Figure 4.12 Results of standard error calculations

The Regression command output in Figure 4.9 has been placed on a sheet called *LR Command* and this is seen in the formula when referencing the Student *t* distribution, the standard error and the number of observations.

To calculate the upper confidence limit in cell D5 only the beginning of the formula is different to the lower confidence limit. In this case the formula begins with =E5+ . . .

The results of these formulae are shown in Figure 4.12 and Figure 4.13 shows the lines plotted onto the graph.

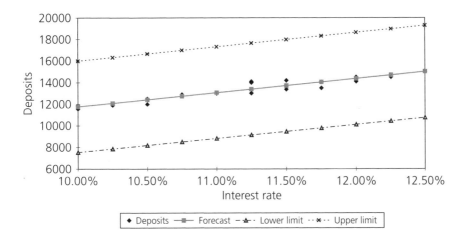

Figure 4.13 Regression line with upper and lower confidence limits

Multiple linear regression

When two or more dependent (*X*) variables are required for a prediction the analysis is referred to as *multiple linear regression*.

The simple linear regression equation can be adapted to accommodate multiple dependent variables in the following way:

$$Y = A_0 + A_1X_1 + A_2X_2 + \cdots + A_nX_n$$

Theoretically there is no limit to the number of independent variables that can be analysed, but within the spreadsheet the maximum is 75. This is a far greater number than would ever actually be required in a business situation.

	A	B	C	D	E	F	G
1	Dependent - X1	Dependent - X2	Independent - Y				
2	Advertising	Sales Promotion	Sales				
3	123	63	900		Estimation of future sales volumes		
4	234	117	1000				
5	321	161	1200		Estimated sales		
6	234	117	1050		Advertising expenditure		
7	231	116	876		Promotion Expenditure		
8	234	117	778				
9	432	216	1550				
10	234	117	777				
11	333	167	678				
12	234	117	876				

Figure 4.14 Multiple regression scenario

The following example in Figure 4.14 represents expenditure on advertising and sales promotion together with sales achieved, where the advertising and sales promotion are dependent variables and the sales achieved is the independent variable. The requirement is to estimate future sales by entering advertising and promotion expenditure, and applying the multiple regression equation to predict the sales value.

In Excel there are no built-in functions for multiple regression and therefore the command method is required. Figure 4.15 shows the

	A	B	C	D	E	F	G	H	I
14	SUMMARY OUTPUT								
15									
16	Regression Statistics								
17	Multiple R	0.616175498							
18	R Square	0.379672245							
19	Adjusted R Squ	0.202435743							
20	Standard Error	226.4243946							
21	Observations	10							
22									
23	ANOVA								
24		df	SS	MS	F	Significance F			
25	Regression	2	219650.4548	109825.2	2.142179	0.1880071			
26	Residual	7	358876.0452	51268.01					
27	Total	9	578526.5						
28									
29		Coefficients	Standard Error	t Stat	P-value	Lower 95%	Upper 95%	Lower 95.0%	Upper 95.0%
30	Intercept	421.2665987	299.2793684	1.407603	0.20207	-286.41615	1128.949	-286.416	1128.949
31	Advertising	-30.5718863	86.26753425	-0.35438	0.733486	-234.56204	173.4183	-234.562	173.4183
32	Sales Promotion	65.18727619	173.4035007	0.375928	0.718104	-344.84655	475.2211	-344.847	475.2211
33									

Figure 4.15 Results of Regression command for multiple linear regression

results of the Excel Regression command where the range C3:C12 from Figure 4.14 was specified as the independent variable and A3:B12 from Figure 4.14 as the dependent variables. The regression output has been placed on the same sheet commencing in cell A14. In order to calculate the estimated sales value in cell G5 the data in cells B30, B31 and B32 shown in Figure 4.15 are required and the formula for cell G5 is:

=(G6*B31)+(G7*B32)+B30

To use this multiple regression model, data must first be entered into cells G6 and G7. Figure 4.16 shows the estimated sales value if the advertising expenditure is 250 and the promotion expenditure is 125.

	A	B	C	D	E	F	G
1	Dependent - X1	Dependent - X2	Independent - Y				
2	Advertising	Sales Promotion	Sales				
3	123	63	900		Estimation of future sales volumes		
4	234	117	1000				
5	321	161	1200		Estimated sales		927
6	234	117	1050		Advertising expenditure		250
7	231	116	876		Promotion Expenditure		125
8	234	117	778				
9	432	216	1550				
10	234	117	777				
11	333	167	678				
12	234	117	876				

Figure 4.16 Results of multiple regression using the command method

Providing the X and Y data does not change, different values can be entered into cells G6 and G7 and the estimated sales value will recalculate correctly. However, because the command method has been used for the regression, if any of the X or Y data changes it will be necessary to execute the Regression command again.

Selecting variables for multiple regression

A problem encountered when applying multiple regression methods in forecasting is deciding which variables to use. In the interests of obtaining as accurate a forecast as possible, it is obvious that all the relevant variables should be included.

However, it is often not feasible to do this, because, apart from the complexity of the resulting equation, the following factors must be considered.

◆ In a forecasting situation the inclusion of variables which do not significantly contribute to the regression merely inflate the error of the resulting prediction.

◆ The cost of monitoring many variables may be very high – so it is advisable to exclude variables that are not contributing significantly.

◆ There is no point including terms that contribute less than the error variance, unless there is strong prior evidence that a particular variable should be included.

◆ For successful forecasting, an equation that is stable over a wide range of conditions is necessary. The smaller the number of variables in the equation, the more stable and reliable the equation.

Summary

Regression analysis is a popular forecasting and estimating technique. Although many users might find the mathematics involved quite difficult, the technique itself is relatively easy to use, especially when a model or template has previously been developed.

However, users who do not understand the underlying mathematics should obtain some assistance in the interpretation of the results.

5

Time Series Analysis

Technology is the acknowledged master, the engine that pulls all the rest along and determines where the future shall be, how fast it shall be attained, what we shall do within it, and who shall prosper, who shall languish, who shall fossilize.

— T. Levitt, *Marketing in an Electronic Age*, 1985.

Introduction

A time series is a set of observations recorded over a period of time. It is a sequence of data that is usually observed at regular intervals.

Time series analysis predicts the value of an item by studying the past movements of that item. It is a series that uses time as the independent or explanatory variable.

Time series data can be analysed for *trend*, *seasonal fluctuations* and *residual*. Trend analysis involves using a linear regression model with time as the independent variable. The data is also adjusted for seasonal fluctuations since this can significantly influence the regression results. The residual is what is left over after the trend and seasonality has been taken into account, and in this case consists of a *cycle* and an *error*.

Many time series follow a cycle, with either an annual or seasonal pattern. These cyclical effects are analysed, as are the errors. This is achieved through *decomposition* analysis.

Decomposition analysis is the method of reducing a set of time series data to a trend, a seasonal factor and a residual. This may be expressed as:

$D = TSR$

where D = data, T = trend, S = seasonality factor and R = residual which includes the error.

The decomposition analysis may be either multiplicative or additive. Additive decomposition takes the following form:

$D = T + S + R$

and multiplicative decomposition analysis takes the form:

$$D = T * S * R$$

The multiplicative model is also referred to as a *ration model*. It is the multiplicative model that is used in this chapter.

Multiplicative time series analysis

The decomposition method described here fits a linear regression line to a set of historic quarterly sales data, establishes the trend, and then uses a centred weighted moving average to isolate the seasonality. The residual from the difference between the data trend and the seasonality is then deduced.

The cyclical component of a series may be estimated by comparing the actual value for each month, with the centred moving average for the month. Since the centred moving average is based on four quarters and is equally weighted with data from, before and after the periods in question, the moving average should be free of seasonal effects and should not be affected by trend.

The de-seasonalised series consists of the historic series, but with the seasonal fluctuations removed. It is a useful aid for judging the overall behaviour of the historic series because the distraction of the seasonal fluctuations has been removed. It is also useful for judging whether one or more values in the historic series deviate appreciably from the general trend. It is important to detect and, if possible, explain such anomalies in order to anticipate potential future recurrences.

The trend describes the long-term behaviour of the series after the removal of the seasonal effects and the irregularities due to short-term random fluctuations. The trend is shown by means of a straight line whose slope indicates the long-term increase or decrease per unit time in the series.

The seasonal component indicates the adjustments that act on the trend due to seasonality. These are expressed as percentages, and repeat themselves in each year.

The residuals are also expressed as percentages. They represent the deviations from the combined series consisting of trend and seasonal components. Allowances are made for the possibility that the residuals may exhibit cyclical behaviour.

A time series analysis model

The development of a time series model requires a moderate amount of statistical knowledge that is beyond the scope of this book to explain in detail. However, the system shown in this chapter is a good example of how a complex application can be developed in such a way that it can be used by less experienced people to great effect. The template on the CD accompanying this book which is called TIMESERIES can be used without amendment to produce quarterly time series forecasts, and readers wishing to examine the theory behind the formulae can study the *Calculation and Processing* worksheet.

The approach to developing the quarterly time series forecasting system is described in this chapter and the model consists of three worksheets which have been called *Data Input and Output*, *Calculation and Processing* and *Graphics*.

Data input and output

The *Data Input and Output* sheet consists of an input form that captures the historic data. The model has been designed to collect historic quarterly data for a three-year period. On the same sheet the final results of the time series analysis are displayed in order that comparisons can be made with the historic data.

Figure 5.1 shows the completed *Data Input and Output* sheet together with some sample data.

	A	B	C	D	E
1	TIME SERIES MULTIPLICATIVE MODEL FOR QUARTERLY DATA				
2					
3	3 YEARS HISTORIC DATA IS REQUIRED TO PRODUCE A FORECAST				
4		Qrt-1	Qrt-2	Qrt-3	Qrt-4
5	Earliest year (T-3)	6500	6950	7200	8500
6	Year after (T-2)	6900	7200	7500	7700
7	Last Year (T-1)	7300	7600	8200	9000
8					
9	RESULTS OF TIME SERIES ANALYSIS				
10		Qrt-1	Qrt-2	Qrt-3	Qrt-4
11	Forecast for T+1	7955.53	8286.13	8684.79	9602.52
12	Forecast for T+2	8424.91	8804.65	9219.89	10185.19
13	Forecast for T+3	8928.49	9323.18	9754.99	10767.85
14					

Figure 5.1 Input and Output worksheet with data

Cells B11 through E13 contain references to cells in the *Calculation and Processing* sheet as no calculations are performed on the *Data Input and Output* sheet. This can be seen in Figure 5.2.

	A	B	C	D
1	TIME SERIES MU			
2				
3	3 YEARS HISTOR			
4		Qrt-1	Qrt-2	Qrt-3
5	Earliest year (T-3)	6500	6950	7200
6	Year after (T-2)	6900	7200	7500
7	Last Year (T-1)	7300	7600	8200
8				
9	RESULTS OF TIM			
10		Qrt-1	Qrt-2	Qrt-3
11	Forecast for T+1	='Calculation and Processing'!B21	='Calculation and Processing'!C21	='Calculation and Processing'!D21
12	Forecast for T+2	='Calculation and Processing'!F21	='Calculation and Processing'!G21	='Calculation and Processing'!H21
13	Forecast for T+3	='Calculation and Processing'!J21	='Calculation and Processing'!K21	='Calculation and Processing'!L21

Figure 5.2 Cell contents for Data Input and Output worksheet

Calculation and processing

The *Calculation and Processing* sheet contains the formulae for decomposing the historic data to establish the trend, seasonality and residual and then to provide the forecast data with standard deviations. Figures 5.3 and 5.4 show the results section of the *Calculation and Processing* sheet, and Figures 5.5 and 5.6 show the

	A	B	C	D	E	F	G
1	CALCULATION AND PROCESSING FOR TIME SERIES ANALYSIS						
2		1	2	3	4	5	6
3	12 periods of quarterly data	Q1	Q2	Q3	Q4	Q5	Q6
4	Historic data	6500	6950	7200	8500	6900	7200
5							
6	Trend	6810.26	6944.00	7077.74	7211.48	7345.22	7478.96
7	Seasonal Components	94.1%	96.9%	100.0%	108.9%	94.1%	96.9%
8	Residual	101.4%	103.3%	101.7%	108.2%	99.8%	99.3%
9	Seasonally adjusted data	6905.20	7170.39	7198.21	7804.12	7330.14	7428.32
10	Trend and seasonally adjusted	6410.62	6730.57	7079.50	7854.52	6914.20	7249.09
11							
12	Forecast period number	13	14	15	16	17	18
13	Forecast quarters	Q13	Q14	Q15	Q16	Q17	Q18
14	Forecast Trend Values	8415.15	8548.89	8682.63	8816.38	8950.12	9083.86
15	Seasonal components	94.1%	96.9%	100.0%	108.9%	94.1%	96.9%
16	Residual components	1.0043	1.0000	1.0000	1.0000	1.0000	1.0000
17							
18	FORECASTS	Q13	Q14	Q15	Q16	Q17	Q18
19	Very Low (-4 STD)	4679.91	5010.51	5409.17	6326.90	5149.29	5529.03
20	Low (-2STD)	6317.72	6648.32	7046.98	7964.71	6787.10	7166.84
21	Mean	7955.53	8286.13	8684.79	9602.52	8424.91	8804.65
22	High (+ 2STD)	9593.34	9923.94	10322.60	11240.33	10062.72	10442.46
23	Very High (+4 STD)	11231.15	11561.75	11960.41	12878.14	11700.53	12080.27

Figure 5.3 Results section of Calculation and Processing worksheet

	A	B	C
1	CALCULATION AND PROCESS		
2		1	=B2+1
3	12 periods of quarterly data	Q1	Q2
4	Historic data	='Input and Output'!B5	='Input and Output'!C5
5			
6	Trend	=FORECAST(B2,$B$4:$M$4,$B$2:$M$2)	=FORECAST(C2,$B$4:$M$4,$B$2:$M$2)
7	Seasonal Components	=$B$32/$B$31	=$C$32/$B$31
8	Residual	=B33	=C33
9	Seasonally adjusted data	=B4/B7	=C4/C7
10	Trend and seasonally adjusted	=B6*B7	=C6*C7
11			
12	Forecast period number	13	=B12+1
13	Forecast quarters	Q13	Q14
14	Forecast Trend Values	=FORECAST(B12,$B$4:$M$4,$B$2:$M$2)	=FORECAST(C12,$B$4:$M$4,$B$2:$M$2)
15	Seasonal components	=$B$32/$B$31	=$C$32/$B$31
16	Residual components	=B34*B39+1	=C34*C39+1
17			
18	FORECASTS	Q13	Q14
19	Very Low (-4 STD)	=B21-4*STDEVA($B$21:$M$21)	=C21-4*STDEVA($B$21:$M$21)
20	Low (-2STD)	=B21-2*STDEVA($B$21:$M$21)	=C21-2*STDEVA($B$21:$M$21)
21	Mean	=B14*B15*B16	=C14*C15*C16
22	High (+ 2STD)	=B21+2*STDEVA($B$21:$M$21)	=C21+2*STDEVA($B$21:$M$21)
23	Very High (+4 STD)	=B21+4*STDEVA($B$21:$M$21)	=C21+4*STDEVA($B$21:$M$21)

Figure 5.4 Formulae for results section of Calculation and Processing worksheet

	A	B	C	D	E	F	G
24	WORK AREA						
25							
26	QUARTERS	Q1	Q2	Q3	Q4	Q5	Q6
27	DATA	6500	6950	7200	8500	6900	7200
28	CENTRED MOVING AVERAGE			7337.5	7418.75	7487.5	7425
29	RESIDUALS			0.981260647	1.145745577	0.921535893	0.96969697
30	SEASONAL COMPONENTS	0.94132	0.969263754	1.000248766	1.089168509	0.94131897	0.969263754
31	CENTRING FACTOR	0.99886					
32	INITIAL SEASONAL ESTIMATES	0.94024	0.968155321	0.9991049	1.087922956		
33	CYCLE*RESIDUAL	1.01394	1.032602723	1.017021029	1.082179829	0.997946791	0.993228463
34	W(X)=RESIDUAL-1	0.01394	0.032602723	0.017021029	0.082179829	-0.00205321	-0.00677154
35	W(X)*W(X)	0.00019	0.001062938	0.000289715	0.006753524	4.21567E-06	4.58537E-05
36	W(X)*W(X-1)		0.000454545	0.000554932	0.001398785	-0.00016873	1.39034E-05
37	SUM(W*W)	0.01697					
38	SUM(W(X)*W(X-1))	0.00525					
39	PHI	0.30953					
40							

Figure 5.5 Work area of Calculation and Processing worksheet

	A	B	C	D	
24	WORK AREA				
25					
26	QUARTERS	Q1	Q2	Q3	
27	DATA	=B4	=C4	=D4	=E4
28	CENTRED MOVING AVERAGE			=1/8*B27+1/4*C27+1/4*D27+1/4*E27+1/8*F27	=1/8*C2
29	RESIDUALS			=D4/D28	=E4/E26
30	SEASONAL COMPONENTS	=$B$32/$B$31	=$C$32/$B$31	=$D$32/$B$31	=$E$32
31	CENTRING FACTOR	=SUM(B32:E32)/4			
32	INITIAL SEASONAL ESTIMATE	=($F$29+$J$29)/2	=($G$29+$K$29)/2	=($H$29+$D$29)/2	=($I$29
33	CYCLE*RESIDUAL	=B4/(B6*B7)	=C4/(C6*C7)	=D4/(D6*D7)	=E4/(E6
34	W(X)=RESIDUAL-1	=B33-1	=C33-1	=D33-1	=E33-1
35	W(X)*W(X)	=B34*B34	=C34*C34	=D34*D34	=E34*E
36	W(X)*W(X-1)		=C34*B34	=D34*C34	=E34*D
37	SUM(W*W)	=SUM(B35:M35)			
38	SUM(W(X)*W(X-1))	=SUM(C36:M36)			
39	PHI	=B38/B37			
40					

Figure 5.6 Formulae for the work area of the Calculation and Processing worksheet

work area required to calculate some of the statistics for which there are no built-in statistical functions.

Rows 6 to 10 of the *Calculation and Processing* sheet decompose the historical data to show the trend, the seasonal components and the residual.

The trend describes the long-term behaviour of the series after removal of the seasonal effects and the irregularities due to short-term random fluctuations. It is described by means of a straight line, the slope of which indicates the long-term rate of increase or decrease per unit time in the series. The trend is computed using the centred moving average calculated in row 28 which has the effect of smoothing out seasonal fluctuations and (to some degree) short-term irregularities.

The seasonal components indicate the adjustments that act on the trend due to seasonality. These are expressed as percentages and show, for example, that if the component for season one is 90% then, on average, the value of the series in season one is 90% of the value indicated by the trend. There are precisely as many different seasonal components as there are seasons in the data and so in this example there are four seasons for this quarterly series. The seasonal components repeat each year.

The residuals are also expressed as percentages and represent the deviations from the combined series consisting of trend and seasonal components. Therefore, for example, if the first historical value is 75.9 units and the trend and seasonal components associated with this point in time are 65.0 and 120% respectively, the corresponding residual is calculated as:

$$75.9/(65.0*120\%) = 0.973 = 97.3\%$$

The mean forecast in row 21 can then be calculated by multiplying the trend by the seasonality by the residual (F=T*S*R), and high and low forecast bounds are calculated in rows 19, 20, 23 and 24.

When developing a complex model such as the one described here, a useful form of documentation is to include a brief description of each row to the right of the plan. This can be seen in column N of the TIMESERIES model.

TECHNIQUE
TIP!

Graphics

Three charts have been created which illustrate the original data and the seasonally adjusted data, the trend and seasonally adjusted data and the trendline, and the forecast together with the lines for plus and minus two and four standard deviations. Figures 5.7, 5.8 and 5.9 are examples of these charts using the sample data from Figure 5.1.

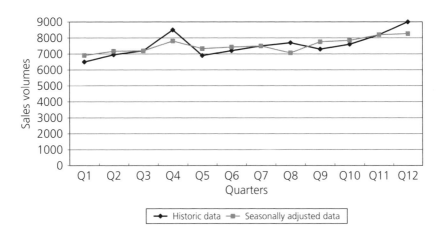

Figure 5.7 Original data and seasonally adjusted data

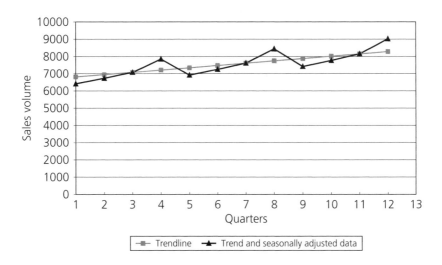

Figure 5.8 Trendline and seasonally adjusted data

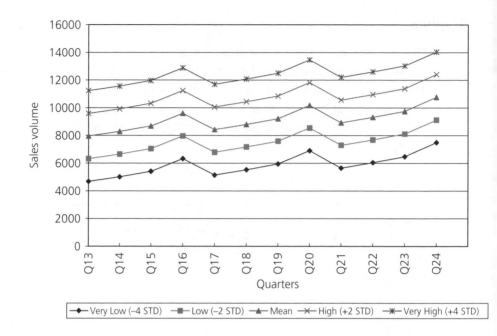

Figure 5.9 Mean forecast and forecast plus and minus two and four standard deviations

Summary

As already stated the formulae required to develop the multiplicative time series template are not trivial and in order to understand the relationships required a sound knowledge of statistics is necessary.

It is beyond the scope of this book to explain in detail all the formulae used, but rather a general overview of the system has been supplied which will allow the reader to work with the template supplied on the accompanying CD.

6

Expected Values

The affair (investment in business) was partly a lottery, though with the ultimate result largely governed by whether the abilities and character of the managers were above or below the average. Some would fail and some would succeed.

– John Maynard Keynes, *The General Theory of Employment, Interest and Money*, 1964.

Introduction

Quantitative approaches to forecasting as illustrated in the previous examples depend heavily on data manipulation, whereas qualitative approaches require the input of human knowledge about the item to be forecast. One such subjective approach to forecasting is that of a *composite of individual estimates using expected values*. The approach is quite different to the techniques so far described in this book because it does not depend only on historic data. The expected value technique requires the opinions of experts as to the likely occurrence of events in the future. These occurrences are estimated in terms of their magnitude as well as in terms of their probability of occurrence.

For example, this technique can be used for the evaluation of the probabilities of future sales where there are a large number of clients who are expected to re-purchase from time to time. Because the data will be estimates of expected sales, it is important that the sales force maintain close and regular contact with clients and prospects in order that they are in a position to prepare useful estimations. It is also important that the sales director responsible for the forecast model is familiar with both the clients and his or her sales team.

A model for analysing expected values

The input required for a model to evaluate the probabilities of future sales is a list of existing clients' and prospects' names, together with estimates of what they are expected to spend on the firms' products over the forecast period. The probability of the sales actually occurring, represented as a percentage value, is entered and the estimated sales value is multiplied by the probability to

EXPECT.XLS

produce the *expected value*. The expected value for all the clients and prospects is totalled and this value is used as the forecast of the total sales revenue for the forecast period.

Figure 6.1 shows the spreadsheet on which the data is entered and the expected values are calculated. This data can be found in the file **EXPECT** on the CD accompanying this book. For the purposes of this example, only a small sample of data has been used, but in a real business situation this would be much larger.

	A	B	C	D	E	F
1	Forecasting System using Expected Values to estimate the value of conference seats booked					
2						
3	Salesperson	Prospect/Client Name	Forecast Sales Value	Probability	Expected Value	
4	JB	International Chemicals	25,000	0.20	5,000	
5	HK	Forward Motors	3,000	0.10	300	
6	LM	Penny Bazaar	43,500	0.80	34,800	
7	PL	Health Care Concern	96,000	0.90	86,400	
8	JB	Futuretown University	25,000	0.50	12,500	
9	HK	Century Bank	26,000	0.50	13,000	
10	LM	Midlands Transport	35,000	0.40	14,000	
11	PL	Flagstone Builders	9,000	0.60	5,400	
12	HK	Superflight Airways	11,000	0.40	4,400	
13	LM	Global Computers	62,000	0.10	6,200	
14	PL	Atlantic Shipping	90,000	0.60	54,000	
15	JB	Gregory Cars	99,500	0.40	39,800	
16	HK	Faraway Travel	24,700	0.50	12,350	
17	PL	Lachlans Book Emporium	56,500	0.80	45,200	
18	JB	Proton	7,100	0.30	2,130	
19	HK	Continental Products	28,400	0.50	14,200	
20	LM	Keepers Bank	30,600	0.40	12,240	
21	PL	Advanced Manufacturing	5,100	0.60	3,060	
22	HK	Biggleswade Institute of Management	20,400	0.80	16,320	
23	LM	Comfee Seats	41,400	0.70	28,980	
24	PL	Findahouse	13,100	0.20	2,620	
25	HK	Fresh Produce	4,300	0.70	3,010	
26	LM	John Doe and Associates	44,700	0.80	35,760	
27	PL	Oscars D-I-Y	90,100	0.20	18,020	
28	JB	PariMax Societe Annomie	44,600	0.30	13,380	
29	HK	Philbys Contractors	2,300	0.80	1,840	
30	PL	Pearl International	30,700	0.90	27,630	
31	JB	Southern Trading Company	59,500	0.20	11,900	
32	HK	Tentacle Manufacturers	10,500	0.60	6,300	
33		Total Expected Sales	1,039,000	0.50	530,740	

Figure 6.1 Model for analysing expected sales values

This technique relies on the fact that with a large list of clients and prospects, the probabilities will average themselves out and the end result will be close to the forecast expected value. The formula for the expected value is:

*Expected value = Forecast value * Probability*

The model does not contain many formulae. A simple multiplication in the Expected value column multiplies the forecast sales value by the probability, and in the totals row the forecast sales and the expected values have been totalled and the probability has been averaged using the =average function.

The totals have been entered using the =subtotal function as opposed the more common =sum function because the =subtotal function allows cells to be totalled subject to a criteria. The formula in cell E33 is =SUBTOTAL(9,E4:E32).

Where 9 means that only cells that are on view are to be summed. The significance of this will become clear in the next section when the list is filtered to show only selected clients and the totals will reflect the totals of the filtered list.

The =subtotal function has options 1–11 which refer to different functions. For example, =SUBTOTAL(1,D4:D32) will average the cells that are on view as opposed to summing them. More information on the use of this function can be found in the Help function within Excel.

Extracting data

Having entered all the data into the spreadsheet it can be used to select subsets of clients based on specified criteria. For example, it might be useful to know the clients who are listed with a probability of more than 0.5.

Excel has a feature called Autofilter that can be used for this purpose. Autofilter is switched on by placing the cursor on any of the cells in the list area (A3:E33 in this example) and selecting DATA FILTER AUTOFILTER. This places a small arrow to the right of each column heading in the expected value table. By clicking on the arrow in the Probability column a series of options are displayed which includes Custom. Figure 6.2 shows the custom dialogue box which allows the required criteria to be entered – in this case 'greater than (>) 0.5'.

The results of the above query can be seen in Figure 6.3. Notice that the rows containing probability values that do not satisfy the criteria are hidden and the totals have been recalculated to reflect the items currently in the list.

	A	B	C	D	E	F
1	Forecasting system using Expected Values to estimate the value of conference seats booked					
2						
3	Salespers ▼	Prospect/Client Name ▼	Forecast Sales Val ▼	Probabil ▼	Expected Val ▼	
4	JB	International Chemicals				
5	HK	Forward Motors				
6	LM	Penny Bazaar				
7	PL	Health Care Concern				
8	JB	Futuretown University				
9	HK	Century Bank				
10	LM	Midlands Transport				
11	PL	Flagstone Builders				
12	HK	Superflight Airways				
13	LM	Global Computers				
14	PL	Atlantic Shipping				
15	JB	Gregory Cars				
16	HK	Faraway Travel				
17	PL	Lachlans Book Emporium				
18	JB	Proton				
19	HK	Continental Products	28,400	0.50	14,200	
20	LM	Keepers Bank	30,600	0.40	12,240	
21	PL	Advanced Manufacturing	5,100	0.60	3,060	
22	HK	Biggleswade Institute of Management	20,400	0.80	16,320	
23	LM	Comfee Seats	41,400	0.70	28,980	

Custom AutoFilter dialog box:

Show rows where:
Probability
is greater than — .5
● And ○ Or

Use ? to represent any single character
Use * to represent any series of characters

OK   Cancel

Probabilities / Criteria / Sheet4 / Sheet5 / Sheet6 / Sheet7 / Sheet8 / Sheet9 / Sheet10

Figure 6.2 Criteria selection dialogue box

	A	B	C	D	E	F	G
1	Forecasting system using Expected Values to estimate the value of conference seats booked						
2							
3	Salespers ▼	Prospect/Client Name ▼	Forecast Sales Val ▼	Probabil ▼	Expected Val ▼		
6	LM	Penny Bazaar	43,500	0.80	34,800		
7	PL	Health Care Concern	96,000	0.90	86,400		
11	PL	Flagstone Builders	9,000	0.60	5,400		
14	PL	Atlantic Shipping	90,000	0.60	54,000		
17	PL	Lachlans Book Emporium	56,500	0.80	45,200		
21	PL	Advanced Manufacturing	5,100	0.60	3,060		
22	HK	Biggleswade Institute of Management	20,400	0.80	16,320		
23	LM	Comfee Seats	41,400	0.70	28,980		
25	HK	Fresh Produce	4,300	0.70	3,010		
26	LM	John Doe and Associates	44,700	0.80	35,760		
29	HK	Philbys Contractors	2,300	0.80	1,840		
30	PL	Pearl International	30,700	0.90	27,630		
32	HK	Tentacle Manufacturers	10,500	0.60	6,300		
33		Total Expected Sales	454,400	0.80	348,700		
34							
35							

Figure 6.3 Results of query on probability greater than 0.5

If a permanent record is required of items satisfying a particular requirement, a report can be produced using the DATA FILTER ADVANCE FILTER command.

On a separate worksheet the column headings should be copied twice – once to be used as a reference for the criteria and once as the headings of the final report. In the example here, all the headings have been copied across, but it is possible to be selective here providing the syntax of the headings matches the column headings on the original list of data. Figure 6.4 shows the prepared worksheet and the dialogue box for the DATA FILTER ADVANCED FILTER command.

The results of the command are shown in Figure 6.5.

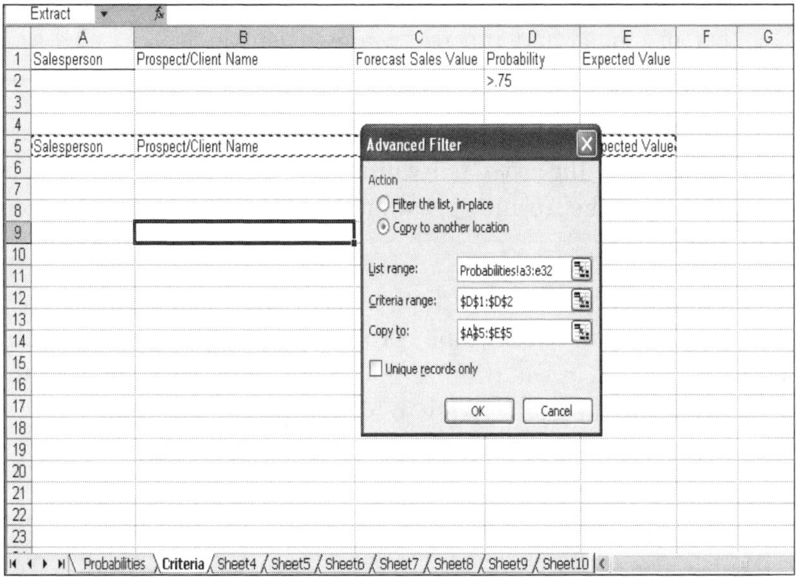

Figure 6.4 Data Filter Advanced Filter command

	A	B	C	D	E	F
1	Salesperson	Prospect/Client Name	Forecast Sales Value	Probability	Expected Value	
2				>.75		
3						
4						
5	Salesperson	Prospect/Client Name	Forecast Sales Value	Probability	Expected Value	
6	LM	Penny Bazaar	43,500	0.80	34,800	
7	PL	Health Care Concern	96,000	0.90	86,400	
8	PL	Lachlans Book Emporium	56,500	0.80	45,200	
9	HK	Biggleswade Institute of Management	20,400	0.80	16,320	
10	LM	John Doe and Associates	44,700	0.80	35,760	
11	HK	Philbys Contractors	2,300	0.80	1,840	
12	PL	Pearl International	30,700	0.90	27,630	
13						
14						
15						
16						
17						

Figure 6.5 A permanent report produced using Data Filter Advanced Filter

OPPORTUNITY
FOR GIGO

It should be noted that the results of this command are not dynamic (rather like the Data Regression command used in an earlier chapter) and thus if the data in the original list is changed, added to or deleted from, this report will not automatically update.

Summary

The composite of individual estimates using expected values technique is particularly useful in situations where there are a large number of clients and prospects, and when there is a sales force who maintains regular and close contact with the client/prospect base.

In these situations, the large number of clients and prospects ensure that the expected value averages out over the whole range, and that the resulting estimation approximately represents the actual sales.

The main problem with this technique is the subjective values involved in setting the probability levels for each client or prospect. If great care is not taken over these figures then the resulting forecast is likely to be of little value.

7

Selecting and Evaluating Forecasting Techniques

> *Real problems are hard to spot, especially for managers so involved in day-to-day operations that they have inadequate perspective to see the big picture.*
>
> — F. Wiersema, *Customer Intimacy*, 1996.

Introduction

This section of the book will explain in some detail how to prepare forecasts using a range of different methods, tools and techniques. For any forecast to be useful it has to be accurate to an acceptable level and the level of accuracy can be affected considerably by the forecasting approach that is taken. This chapter provides a table of different forecasting techniques and indicates when they might be suitable. Some guidelines are given as to how to measure the level of accuracy after a forecast has been calculated.

Selecting the right technique

Table 7.1 provides a list of the forecasting techniques described in this book and evaluates them under the following sections:

◆ appropriate use
◆ time horizon
◆ maths sophistication
◆ data required.

Table 7.1 Different forecasting techniques

Technique	Use	Maths	Data
Moving averages	Repeated forecasts without seasonality	A minimal level of competency	Historic data essential
Adaptive filtering	Repeated forecasts without seasonality and where the nature of any trend may change over time	Some statistical knowledge is required	Historic data essential, but level and detail can vary

Continued

Table 7.1 Different forecasting techniques—cont'd

Technique	Use	Maths	Data
Exponential smoothing	Repeated forecast with or without seasonality	Some statistical knowledge to set up a system but virtually none to operate a well-designed system	Only recent data and current forecast is required once the smoothing factor is established
Simple linear regression	Comparing one independent variable with one dependent variable where there is a linear relationship between the variables	Some statistical knowledge to set up a system but virtually none to operate a well-designed system	A sample of relevant observations for the independent and dependent variables
Multiple linear regression	When more than one independent variables is to be compared with a dependent variable	Some statistical knowledge is required	A sample of relevant observations for the independent and dependent variables
Trend analysis	Forecasting over time in a non-linear way using simple regression	Some statistical competence is required	Historic data with as much detail as possible
Decomposition analysis	Identify seasonal components as part of another forecasting method	Requires statistical knowledge to set up a system but virtually none to operate a well-designed system	Historic data for the one variable under consideration is required
Composite of individual estimates	Forecasting using a large number of individual estimates	No statistics and only basic arithmetic required	Past data not required

The techniques described are not an exhaustive list of forecasting techniques, but cover those most suited to the spreadsheet environment, and which have already been explained in this book.

Accuracy and reliability

Every forecast should include an estimate of its accuracy and an assessment of its reliability. This not only allows for a reasonable and acceptable margin of error, but also helps to build confidence in the methods being used, and the results achieved.

Many forecasts are repetitive, being prepared either weekly or monthly. This provides an invaluable source of forecast assessment data, since the forecasts can be measured against the reality, and can then be adjusted with the benefit of hindsight. Explicit analysis will highlight weak spots in the forecast, and improve the accuracy of future forecasts.

The three primary approaches to evaluating the accuracy of a forecast are to use charts, supported by quantitative (statistical) analysis and subjective methods.

Charts

Charts are particularly useful when it is necessary to identify potential problems as early as possible. Control charts are the most frequently used graphical method, and these are useful for identifying when a forecast method requires adjustment. Prediction realisation diagrams are another graphical method to consider. The pictorial representation of the data makes it easier to spot changes in data patterns and can direct the analyst to the data areas that need to be examined.

Statistical methods

Quantitative or statistical methods are useful for comparing different forecasting methods, and in estimating confidence limits. A confidence limit is a specification that combines a statement about a point estimate with a measure of the precision of that estimate. Some useful statistical measures that have been used in the models in this section include the following.

Average error

The *average error*, or the *average absolute error* or the *mean absolute error*, is the simplest of all to compute. The algebraic formula is:

$$Average\ error = (|\ (F_1 - A_1)\ | + |\ (F_2 + A_2)\ | + \cdots$$

$$+ |\ (F_t - A_t)\ |)/T$$

where F_t = forecast for period t, A_t = actual value for period t, T = number of forecasts to be used and the modulus (|) means that the absolute value is to be used. In other words if the value is negative, its sign should be changed to positive.

Once computed, the average error for a particular forecasting method can be compared with the average error for another method. Alternatively, the average error for different time periods can be calculated and compared. Although the average error does not have any intrinsic statistical property that makes it useful for the estimation of confidence limits, it is a useful indication as to the accuracy of a forecast.

Standard error

The most widely used measure of forecasting accuracy is the standard error and this technique was used in Chapter 4 in conjunction with the regression analysis.

The standard error is particularly useful because it can be used to compute confidence limits and, because the terms are squared, it places more emphasis on large errors. There are however some pre-requisites for the use of standard errors:

♦ The error terms are normally distributed. A normal distribution is a model of a continuous variable whose value depends upon the effect of a number of factors, each factor exerting a small positive or negative influence.
♦ The average forecasting error is zero, i.e. there is no tendency to regularly over or under-estimate.
♦ The errors are not serially correlated, i.e. the error terms do not show a pattern, in terms of direction or size, over time.

If all these conditions are met, then 68% of the outcomes will be within plus or minus one standard error, 95% will be within plus or minus twice the standard error and 99.7% will be within plus or minus three times the standard error.

The control chart will show whether there is any pattern in the error terms, and calculation of the error terms will show whether they meet the necessary conditions as a basis for computation of the confidence limits.

Thiels *U*

Thiels *U* compares the accuracy of a forecasting model to a naïve model that uses the last period's outcome to predict the present period's outcome. This is using what is already known to predict the future and is thus a measure of relative accuracy. *U* is defined by:

$$U = \frac{\text{Standard error of forecasting model}}{\text{Standard error of naïve model}}$$

Values of *U* greater than one indicate that the method of forecasting selected was worse than the naïve model; values less than one indicate that it was better.

U can also be used to compare the accuracy of various forecasting methods, or even to compare the accuracy of one method over different time-spans. This is useful when selecting the optimum time-span or period for a forecast.

Subjective methods

Subjective forecasting methods are based on common sense. They involve using a measure of judgement and self-expertise in the evaluation of a forecast.

When applying subjective methods it is important to avoid *spurious correlations* which refers to correlations where the associations are real enough, but misinterpretation of the results, or unwise jumping to conclusions, has led to erroneous conclusions being drawn from the forecast.

The original assumptions under which the predictions were made, and upon which the model was built, should be kept in mind. If a factor is considered to be particularly critical, then different fore-casts can be prepared using alternative assumptions.

No matter how well the forecast has performed in the past, the model itself and its underlying assumptions should be periodi-cally re-examined in order to ensure that the same conditions prevail.

Summary

As success at forecasting is an important contributor to the firm's performance, time and effort should be applied to ensure that a suitable forecasting technique is being used. This will certainly result in costs of various types being minimised.

All three methods discussed in this chapter are important and can be applied individually or collectively depending on the precise situation.

Part 2

Business Planning

Planning, of course is not a separate, recognizable act . . . . Every managerial act, mental or physical is inexorably intertwined with planning. It is as much a part of every managerial act as breathing is to the living human.

– C. George, *The History of Management*, 1972.

Introduction

Business forecasting involves the prediction of what could happen in the future and business planning involves the calculation of what is required to fulfil the forecast, i.e. make the future happen as it is forecast. Thus a business plan uses a forecast as an initial point of departure and then adds the detail to reflect how the particular process or project is intended to proceed. Business plans are generally set in the future and involve making a series of assumptions about how the variables in the plan will behave in future periods.

Business plans are helpful with the decision-making process of an organisation. There are many types of business plan, which range from simple verbal or written descriptions of what is to be achieved, through diagrammatic representations such as Gantt charts to highly analytical numeric reports.

There are many definitions of planning, but perhaps one worth quoting is from Ackoff[1] who said:

> Planning is required when the future state that we desire involves a set of interdependent decisions; that is, a system of decisions . . . The principal complexity in planning derives from the interrelatedness of the decisions rather than from the decisions themselves . . .

In the context of this book, a business plan is a statement of quantifiable objectives, together with the resources required to achieve them. The objective may be profit, market share, return on investment or cash flow, to mention only a few, and the resources could be manpower, materials, capital, cash, etc.

There are many different ways of classifying business plans, including short-term plans, long-term plans, profit plans, marketing plans, production plans, personnel development plans, capital

---

[1] R.L. Ackoff, *A Concept of Corporate Planning*, Wiley, New York, 1970.

investment plans, merger and take-over plans, etc. The level of analysis in the plan reflects the ultimate use for which it is intended. For high-level strategic decisions, plans generally do not contain very much detail, while for operational planning a large amount of detail is required. The contents will reflect the nature of the project or process being planned, but it is not unusual for operational plans to involve dozens of line items. These types of plan often form the basis of a financial budget, which in some cases is no more than a plan divided into specific responsibility points and specific time periods.

An important aspect of business planning is *what-if analysis*. This is a process of changing one or more of the variables or assumptions on which a business plan has been based in order to see what effect such a change in circumstances would have on the results. This subject is covered in detail in Chapter 12.

Approaches to business planning

There are three generically different approaches to developing business plans, which are described as *deterministic*[2], *stochastic*[3] or *probabilistic* and *optimising*.

Deterministic planning

Deterministic planning is the most frequently encountered. It is the basis on which virtually all corporate planning and budgeting is performed. A deterministic plan takes single values that are the best estimate for the variables in the plan and uses this value with a set of logic rules to produce the plan or budget. The single start value for a line item in a plan is referred to as a *point estimate*. This might be the result of a forecasting model, and although it is recognised by planners and budgeting officers that accurate point estimates are almost impossible to obtain, it is usually possible to derive a value that is accurate enough to be useful.

---

[2] According to the *American Heritage Dictionary of the English Language*, Third Edition, deterministic refers to the fact that there is an inevitable consequence of antecedents.
[3] According to the *American Heritage Dictionary of the English Language*, Third Edition, stochastic refers to involving a random variable or variables and the chance or probability of their occurrence.

The method of planning is called 'deterministic' because once the point estimates are derived, the outcome of the plan may be uniquely determined by the logic, i.e. there will be only one answer. For example, consider the following:

Sales volume   200
Unit price   20
Revenue   4000 (Sales volume * Unit price)

The only way a different result can be obtained in the above example is by changing one or both of the single point estimates, i.e. the data for the sales volume and the unit price. Of course, one of the great advantages of the spreadsheet is that making changes to opening data, growth rates, cost factors, etc. causes all directly and indirectly affected cells to recalculate and thus different scenarios can be calculated. However, the basic principle is that the outcome is uniquely determined by the logic.

Figure 8.1 is a profit and loss account for CWL that has been developed as a deterministic plan. Figure 8.2 shows the formulae used for the plan.

	A	B	C	D	E	F	G	H
1	Profit and Loss Account for CWL for 4 Quarterly periods							
2								
3		1st qtr	2nd qtr	3rd qtr	4th qtr	Total		
4								
5	No. course attendees	1200	1212	1224	1236	4872		
6	Avg conference fee	250.00	250.00	250.00	250.00			
7	Sales Turnover	300000	303000	306030	309090	1218120		
8								
9	Venue costs	120000	121200	122412	123636	487248		
10	Documentation	12000	12120	12241	12364	48725		
11	Catering	96000	96960	97930	98909	389798		
12	Total Direct Costs	228000	230280	232583	234909	925771		
13								
14	Gross Profit	72000	72720	73447	74181	292348		
15								
16	Administration	3750	3788	3825	3864	15227		
17	Travel	3000	3030	3060	3091	12181		
18	Salary Expenses	12000	12000	12000	12000	48000		
19	Total Other Costs	18750	18818	18886	18955	75408		
20								
21	Net Profit B.T.	53250	53903	54561	55227	216941		
22								
23	Sales growth	1%						
24	Venue costs per attendee	100						
25	Documentation per attendee	10						
26	Catering per attendee	80						
27								
28	Admin as percentage of sales	1.25%						
29	Travel as percentage of sales	1%						
30	Salary growth rate	0%						
31								

CWL-P AND L.XLS

Figure 8.1 A typical deterministic plan

	A	B	C	D	E	F
1	Profit and Loss Account for CWL for 4 Quarterly periods					
2						
3		1st qtr	2nd qtr	3rd qtr	4th qtr	Total
4						
5	No. course attendees	1200	=B5*(1+$B$23)	=C5*(1+$B$23)	=D5*(1+$B$23)	=SUM(B5:E5)
6	Avg conference fee	250	=B6	=C6	=D6	
7	Sales Turnover	=B5*B6	=C5*C6	=D5*D6	=E5*E6	=SUM(B7:E7)
8						
9	Venue costs	=B5*$B$24	=C5*$B$24	=D5*$B$24	=E5*$B$24	=SUM(B9:E9)
10	Documentation	=B5*$B$25	=C5*$B$25	=D5*$B$25	=E5*$B$25	=SUM(B10:E10)
11	Catering	=B5*$B$26	=C5*$B$26	=D5*$B$26	=E5*$B$26	=SUM(B11:E11)
12	Total Direct Costs	=ROUND(SUM(B9:B11),0)	=ROUND(SUM(C9:C11),0)	=ROUND(SUM(D9:D11),0)	=ROUND(SUM(E9:E11),0)	=ROUND(SUM(F9:F1
13						
14	Gross Profit	=B7-B12	=C7-C12	=D7-D12	=E7-E12	=SUM(B14:E14)
15						
16	Administration	=B7*$B$28	=C7*$B$28	=D7*$B$28	=E7*$B$28	=SUM(B16:E16)
17	Travel	=B7*$B$29	=C7*$B$29	=D7*$B$29	=E7*$B$29	=SUM(B17:E17)
18	Salary Expenses	12000	=B18*(1+$B$30)	=C18*(1+$B$30)	=D18*(1+$B$30)	=SUM(B18:E18)
19	Total Other Costs	=SUM(B16:B18)	=SUM(C16:C18)	=SUM(D16:D18)	=SUM(E16:E18)	=SUM(B19:E19)
20						
21	Net Profit B.T.	=B14-B19	=C14-C19	=D14-D19	=E14-E19	=SUM(B21:E21)
22						
23	Sales growth	0.01				
24	Venue costs per attendee	100				
25	Documentation per attendee	10				
26	Catering per attendee	80				
27						
28	Admin as percentage of sales	0.0125				
29	Travel as percentage of sales	0.01				
30	Salary growth rate	0				
31						

Figure 8.2 Formulae for the deterministic plan

The example shown above is a profit and loss account for a profit-making organisation. However, the deterministic approach to business planning is equally applied to not-for-profit situations when an organisation might be planning, for example, an allocation of funds. Figure 8.3 is such an example.

CHARITY.XLS

	A	B	C	D	E	F	G	H
1	**Charity Shop**							
2		Jan	Feb	Mar	Apr	May	Jun	Total
3	**Expenses**							
4	Rent	500	500	500	500	500	500	3000
5	community charge	60	60	60	60	60	60	360
6	Honoraria	600	600	600	600	600	600	3600
7	Electricity	100	100	100	100	100	100	600
8	Water	50	50	50	50	50	50	300
9	Teas/Cleaning	15	15	15	15	15	15	90
10	Advertising	25	25	25	25	25	25	150
11	**Total Expenses**	**1350**	**1350**	**1350**	**1350**	**1350**	**1350**	**8100**
12								
13	**Revenue**							
14	Sales	5000	5000	5000	5000	5000	5000	30000
15	Donations	500	500	500	500	500	500	3000
16	Subscriptions	75	75	75	75	75	75	450
17	**Total revenue**	**5575**	**5575**	**5575**	**5575**	**5575**	**5575**	**33450**
18								
19	*Surplus/Deficit*	*4225*	*4225*	*4225*	*4225*	*4225*	*4225*	*25350*
20								

Figure 8.3 Allocation of funds plan

Stochastic planning

A stochastic or probabilistic plan recognises that because point estimates are difficult to accurately establish, it is can be preferable to establish ranges into which it is thought values will fall. For example, in a stochastic plan, rather than using a point estimate of £50,000 as an opening sales value, a range consisting of values of between, say £45,000 and £52,500 could be entered. Similar ranges could be entered for other line items in the plan.

Probabilities are then associated with the data input ranges and the computer recalculates the plan thousands of times using values within the specified range to produce a large number of results, or scenarios, which correspond to different possible outcomes. This method is referred to as the *Monte Carlo* method. It is frequently used to evaluate large capital investment alternatives of complex marketing situations. Because this type of planning is concerned with attributing the probability of a particular outcome, it is also referred to as *risk analysis*.

There are a number of different probability distribution techniques that can be applied to stochastic planning, including uniform, triangular and beta. The examples shown in this book will assume a uniform, or normal, distribution. This implies that when the computer generates input data there is an equal chance of any value within the specified range being selected. The other distributions mentioned, i.e. triangular and beta distributions do not have this uniform probability pattern.

Because stochastic planning requires a reiterative process to collect thousands of alternative results, it requires considerable computing power that was not used to be available on desk-top computers and thus was not considered a spreadsheet application. However, with the speed and capacity of the PC today, stochastic planning has become a relatively simple application to develop.

The detail of how to set up and work with a stochastic plan for risk analysis is given in Chapter 13, but the underlying logic required to apply stochastic analysis to the deterministic plan shown in Figure 8.5 using a uniform or normal distribution is as follows:

No. course attendees	*Random * (max − min) + min*
Avg. conference fee	*Random * (max − min) + min*
Revenue	*Attendees * Fee*

The input data for the above model might be:

	Max	*Min*
No. course attendees	1200	800
Avg. conference fee	250	175

The use of a random selection from the ranges provides a normal, uniform or rectangular distribution, but other distributions such as binomial, poisson or triangular could be specified.

Figure 8.4 shows a typical data input form for a stochastic plan and Figure 8.5 shows some of the formulae required. The results of risk analysis are usually best viewed graphically and an example is shown in Figure 8.6.

CWL-RISK.XLS

	A	B	C	D	E	F
1	**Profit and Loss Account for CWL for 4 Quarterly periods**					
2						
3	Input for stochastic planning					
4		*Max*	*Min*			
5						
6	No. course attendees	1200	800			
7	Avg conference fee	250.00	175.00			
8						
9						

Figure 8.4 Input form for risk analysis

	A	B	C	
1	**Profit and Loss Account for**			
2				
3		*1st qtr*	*2nd qtr*	
4				
5	No. course attendees	=INT(RAND()*(Input!B6-Input!C6)+Input!C6)	=B5*(1+$B$23)	=C5*(1+$B
6	Avg conference fee	=INT(RAND()*(Input!B7-Input!C7)+Input!C7)	=B6	=C6
7	**Sales Turnover**	=B5*B6	=C5*C6	=D5*D6
8				
9	Venue costs	=B5*$B$24	=C5*$B$24	=D5*$B$24
10	Documentation	=B5*$B$25	=C5*$B$25	=D5*$B$25
11	Catering	=B5*$B$26	=C5*$B$26	=D5*$B$26
12	**Total Direct Costs**	=ROUND(SUM(B9:B11),0)	=ROUND(SUM(C9:C11),0)	=ROUND(S
13				
14	***Gross Profit***	=B7-B12	=C7-C12	=D7-D12
15				
16	Administration	=B7*$B$28	=C7*$B$28	=D7*$B$28
17	Travel	=B7*$B$29	=C7*$B$29	=D7*$B$29
18	Salary Expenses	12000	=B18*(1+$B$30)	=C18*(1+$
19	***Total Other Costs***	=SUM(B16:B18)	=SUM(C16:C18)	=SUM(D16
20				
21	**Net Profit B.T.**	=B14-B19	=C14-C19	=D14-D19
22				
23	Sales growth	0.01		
24	Venue costs per attendee	100		
25	Documentation per attendee	10		
26	Catering per attendee	80		
27				
28	Admin as percentage of sales	0.0125		
29	Travel as percentage of sales	0.01		
30	Salary growth rate	0		

Figure 8.5 Formulae required for risk analysis

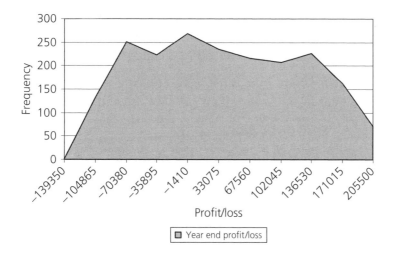

Figure 8.6 Graph showing results of risk analysis

From the graph in Figure 8.6 it can be seen that, given all the assumptions in the underlying model, the most likely outcome is a net profit of about £20,000. However, given the ranges of input data it is possible for there to be a net loss of £139,350 or there could possibly be a profit as high as £205,000.

There are a number of factors that need to be taken into consideration when interpreting the results of a stochastic plan and this is discussed in more detail in Chapter 13.

Optimising models

Optimising models attempt to find a unique course of action that will produce the best result, given a set of restraints. One of the most frequently encountered optimising models in business is the economic order quantity (EOQ) model, whereby the most cost-effective order quantities are calculated. An optimising model always attempts to match an objective within a given set of restraints and the spreadsheet *Solver* feature makes this type of analysis possible within the spreadsheet environment.

Backward iteration or goal seeking is another optimising technique whereby the computer calculates the course of action that should be undertaken in order to achieve a particular objective. In this case, it is usual to change only one variable at a time and constraints are not always necessary. In Excel the *Goal Seek* command can be applied for this type of analysis. Both *Solver* and *Goal Seek* are discussed in more detail in Chapter 12.

Table 8.1 shows the three types of business plans discussed in this chapter together with their primary use and development features.

Table 8.1 Summary of business planning approaches

Type of plan	Primary use	Features
Deterministic	Income and expenditure, budgeting	Extrapolation of formulae and constraints
Risk or stochastic	Complex capital investment appraisal	Exploration of multiple scenarios
Optimising	Finding the unique course of action to produce the optimal result	Solving a series of equations representing operational constraints

Summary

Before embarking on the development of any spreadsheet application it is important to take time to consider what type of plan is required and the best approach for the design and structure of the plan. The following chapters in this book describe the techniques required for the development of deterministic, stochastic and optimising models, as well as how to get the most out of the plans through what-if analysis.

9

Spreadsheet Skills for all Types of Planning

The most popularly claimed pitfall of planning concerns commitment. The assumption is that with the support and participation of the top management, all will be well. But the questions must be asked: well with what and well for whom? For planners? To be sure. But for the organisation?

– Henry Mintzberg, *The Rise and Fall of Strategic Planning*, 1994.

Introduction

Whether a spreadsheet is being developed as a forecasting plan, a profit and loss account or a marketing plan it is essential that due care and attention be given to the design and structure of the plan. Establishing some rules as to how all the spreadsheets in a department or organisation are developed enables different people to look at different plans and feel familiar with the layout, style, reports, charts, etc. This is in much the same way as users feel familiar with software applications that have a similar interface such as those in the Microsoft Office suite of products.

The objectives of good design in spreadsheet terms are exactly the same as those required for any other software development:

◆ To ensure that the spreadsheet is as error free as possible
◆ To ensure that the spreadsheet can be used without much training or control
◆ To minimise the work required to enhance or change the spreadsheet.

If care is taken to ensure sound structure and good design, a spreadsheet will be straightforward to develop, easy to read, simple to use, not difficult to change and will produce the required results.

The plan developed over a number of developmental stages in this chapter illustrates a variety of aspects of the principles of spreadsheet design and development. The series begins with a plan that has had little or no thought put into its design and layout, and as the chapter proceeds ways of improving and enhancing the plan are identified and explained. These plans can be found on the CD accompanying the book under the names STYLE01 through STYLE10.

Spreadsheet 1: Getting started

The spreadsheet in Figure 9.1 is a simple profit projection that may be of use to the author, but is unlikely to be helpful to anyone else. This is clearly a quick one-off plan which has been prepared with very little care and which may well not even be saved on the disk.

STYLE01.XLS

	A	B	C	D	E
1	sales	150	173	198	228
2	price	12.55	12.55	12.55	12.55
3	revenue	1883	2165	2490	2863
4	costs	1185	1362	1567	1802
5	profit	698	803	923	1061
6					

Figure 9.1 Simple profit projection

Problems with this spreadsheet

The immediately obvious problems with this spreadsheet are that it has no title, it is not clear what the columns represent, i.e. they are different periods or perhaps different products, and the author is unknown.

With regards the data itself, the figures are hard to read as there are varying numbers of decimal places. Whilst perhaps there has been a growth in sales and price, the percentage has not been indicated. The costs line could be misleading as no indication of where the costs have been derived is supplied.

Positive aspects of this spreadsheet

If the author of the spreadsheet required a quick profit estimation based on known data and growth rates for sales units, price and costs then the spreadsheet has supplied that information quickly and in a more concise form than would have been achievable using a calculator and recording the results on a paper.

Spreadsheet 2: Ownership and version

In Figure 9.2 the three major shortfalls of the first spreadsheet have been remedied. The plan has also been given a title and author details have been included. It is important that every business plan have a clear owner who is responsible for overseeing the accuracy and maintenance of the system. A name plus some form of contact details should always be included.

	A	B	C	D	E	F	G	H	I
1	Profit Projection for Widget Division for 20XX						Last updated:	Jan 20XX	
2		Written by P.A. Jones							
3		pajones@business.com							
4		0118 999 9999							
5									
6									
7		Qtr 1	Qtr 2	Qtr 3	Qtr 4				
8	sales	150	175	195	220				
9	price	12.55	12.55	12.55	12.55				
10	revenue	1882.5	2196.25	2447.25	2761				
11	costs	1184.55	1381.975	1539.915	1737.34				
12	profit	697.95	814.275	907.335	1023.66				
13									
14									
15									
16									

STYLE02.XLS

Figure 9.2 Incorporating some annotation

Problems with this spreadsheet

The construction of the data and results is still unclear and the lack of formatting makes the figures hard to read. The costs remain grouped together.

Positive aspects of this spreadsheet

In addition to the owner details having been added to the plan, the date when the plan was written is a useful feature. The date becomes particularly important when the question of spreadsheet versions arise. Note that the date has been entered here as text. If a date function had been used, it would be continually updated each time the file is retrieved, whereas here it is the date of the last update that is required. The ruling lines above and below specific sections of the spreadsheet are also quite helpful. This can be quickly achieved using the automatic formatting features. These are accessed via the FORMAT AUTOFORMAT command.

Spreadsheet 3: Formatting

In Figure 9.3 the data for the four quarters is totalled and reported as an annual figure. The values in the plan have also been formatted with the majority of figures being formatted to zero decimal places and the price line to two decimal places.

STYLE03.XLS

	A	B	C	D	E	F	G	H	I
1	Profit Projection for Widget Division for 20XX						Last updated:	Jan 20XX	
2	Written by P.A. Jones								
3	pajones@business.com								
4	0118 999 9999								
5									
6		Qtr 1	Qtr 2	Qtr 3	Qtr 4	Total			
7	sales	150	173	198	228	749			
8	price	12.55	12.55	12.55	12.55				
9	revenue	1883	2165	2490	2863	9400			
10	costs	1185	1362	1567	1802	5915			
11	profit	698	803	923	1061	3485			
12									
13									
14	Report Printed		22-Mar-05	12:29:57					
15									
16									
17									
18									
19									

Figure 9.3 Formatting the plan

One of the automatic formatting options has been selected to shade and outline the plan.

Problems with this spreadsheet

By looking at the plan in Figure 9.3 it can be seen that the sales and the costs both increase over time. However it is not clear by how much because the sales growth factor and the increase in costs have been incorporated into the formulae as absolute references.

OPPORTUNITY
FOR GIGO

The inclusion of absolute values in formulae is not recommended and can lead to GIGO. To change the sales growth factor in Figure 9.3 two processes are required. First, cell C7 is accessed and the edit key is pressed. The growth factor is changed and enter is pressed. This has changed the formula in this one cell, but only once the formula has been extrapolated across into cells D7 and D7 is the amendment complete. It is not difficult to see that there is room for error here in a number of different ways.

Positive aspects of this spreadsheet

Having a current date and time indicator displayed on the spreadsheet ensures that a hard copy report will reflect the date, and perhaps more importantly the time it was printed. This is achieved through the NOW() function, which can be formatted with a range of different display options. Because it is likely that a spreadsheet will be recalculated, even if it is set to manual calculation, before printing, the date and time will always be up to date. It is of course possible to include the date and time in headers and footers, but during the development phase of a system the page layout is of less relevant than printing the section being worked on and so thought should be given to the positioning of the NOW() function.

The cells in this plan have now been formatted, which makes the data easier to read. When formatting a spreadsheet it is important to consider the entire plan and not just the cells that are currently being worked on. The entire spreadsheet should be formatted to the degree of accuracy the majority of the plan is to be and those cells that need to be different, such as percentages, can be reformatted when necessary. This is quickly achieved by right clicking on the top left corner of the spreadsheet at the intersection between the column letters and row numbers and then select format cells. Whatever formatting is now applied will affect the entire worksheet.

It is important to understand that formatting cells only changes the display and does not affect the results of calculations that are still performed to the full degree of accuracy, which is usually 16 significant decimal places. This is why a cell containing the sum of a range of cells might display an answer that does not agree with the result of visually adding the values in the range.

The ROUND function is the only safe way to ensure that the results of a calculation are actually rounded to a given number of decimal places. Figure 9.4 shows two tables representing the same extract from a profit and loss account. In both cases all the cells have been formatted to zero decimal places, but in Table B the ROUND function has been incorporated in the formulae for cells F15 through F19.

	A	B	C	D	E	F
14	Costs					
15	Administration	1500	1576	1656	1739	6471
16	Depreciation	1500	1553	1607	1663	6322
17	Finance Charges	1200	1288	1382	1482	5352
18	Maintenance	600	630	662	696	2588
19	Salary Expenses	13000	13858	14773	15748	57378
20	*Total Other Costs*	17800	18904	20079	21328	78112
21						
22	**Net Profit B.T.**	200	1102	2060	3076	6438
23						

Table A – Formatting only

	A	B	C	D	E	F
14	Costs					
15	Administration	1500	1576	1656	1739	6471
16	Depreciation	1500	1553	1607	1663	6322
17	Finance Charges	1200	1288	1382	1482	5352
18	Maintenance	600	630	662	696	2588
19	Salary Expenses	13000	13858	14773	15748	57378
20	*Total Other Costs*	17800	18904	20079	21328	78111
21						
22	**Net Profit B.T.**	200	1102	2060	3076	6438
23						

Table B – Using ROUND Function

Figure 9.4 Difference between rounding and formatting cells

The formula entered into cell F15, which can then be copied for the other line items is:

=ROUND(SUM(B15:E15),0)

The effect of the ROUND function can be seen in cell F20. By visually adding up the numbers in the range F15 through F19 the result is 78,111 whereas the formatting of these cells without the use of the ROUND function in Table A returns a value of 78,112 in cell F20. Having applied the ROUND function to a cell any future reference made to that cell will use the rounded value.

Excel does offer an alternative to the ROUND function in the Precision as displayed option within TOOLS OPTIONS CALCULATION. This command assumes that calculations will be performed to the level of accuracy currently displayed. The danger of using this command is that when data is changed or added to the spreadsheet the command is no longer valid and it is then necessary to repeat the command to update the spreadsheet – this is another invitation to GIGO.

OPPORTUNITY
FOR GIGO

Spreadsheet 4: Documentation

Spreadsheet developers are notoriously bad at supplying documentation and other supporting information about the plan. There are a number of features offered by Excel to assist in the documenting of plans including the INSERT COMMENT command. Figure 9.5 shows a comment being entered onto a plan – notice how the user name of the comment author is included. This is useful when a team of people are working on a system. The presence of a comment is indicated by a small red triangle on the cell. To read the comment move the cursor over the cell and it will automatically be displayed. A word of caution concerning the use of comment boxes – they take up a considerable amount of space and if used widely they can make a noticeable difference to the size of a file. To clear all the comments use the EDIT CLEAR COMMENTS command.

STYLE04.XLS

	A	B	C	D	E	F	G	H	I
1	Profit Projection for Widget Division for 20XX						Last updated:	Jan 20XX	
2	Written by P.A. Jones								
3	pajones@business.com								
4	0118 999 9999								
5									
6		Qtr 1	Qtr 2	Qtr 3	Qtr 4	Total			
7	sales	150	173	198	228	749			
8	price	12.55	12.55	Sue Nugus:					
9	revenue	1883	2165	This period should be		9400			
10	costs	1185	1362	watched		5915			
11	profit	698	803			3485			
12									
13									
14	Report Printed		22-Mar-05	12:29:57					
15									
16									
17									

Figure 9.5 Inserting comments

The provision of a hard copy report showing the logic used to create a plan is also helpful as this is the ultimate reference point if a formula has been overwritten and needs to be reconstructed.

In Excel there is a shortcut key to display the formulae which is CTRL + ` (accent grave). Alternatively, this can be achieved through the TOOLS OPTIONS VIEW command and then check the Formulas box.

TECHNIQUE TIP!

In addition to providing documentation for a spreadsheet system, looking at the contents of the cells as opposed to the results can also be a helpful auditing tool. For example, Figure 9.6 highlights

	A	B	C	D	E	F
1						
2			Written by P.A. Jones			
3			pajones@business.com			
4			0118 999 9999			
5						
6			Qtr 1	Qtr 2	Qtr 3	Qtr 4	Total
7	sales	150	=B7*1.15	=C7*1.15	=D7*1.15	=SUM(B7:E7)
8	price	12.55	12.55	12.55	12.55	
9	revenue	=B7*B8	=C7*C8	=D7*D8	=E7*E8	=SUM(B9:E9)
10	costs	=B7*7.897	=C7*7.897	=D7*7.897	=E7*7.897	=SUM(B10:E10)
11	profit	=B9-B10	=C9-C10	=D9-D10	=E9-E10	=SUM(B11:E11)
12						
13						
14	Report Printed		=NOW()	=NOW()		
15						
16						
17						
18						
19						

Figure 9.6 Report showing formulae

the fact that there are still values embedded in formulae which is not good practice and is addressed in the next version of the plan.

A third form of documentation which can be particularly useful for large systems is the 'sentence at the end of the row' technique. Requiring less file space than comment boxes, and always on view it can be useful to have a brief description of the activity taking place in each row of a plan.

Spreadsheet 5: Minimising absolute values

One of the reasons that spreadsheets have become such an integral part of the way we do business is the fact that they facilitate quick, easy and inexpensive what-if analysis. What-if analysis may be defined as the process of investigating the effect of changes to assumptions on the objective function of a business plan.

Performing what-if analysis on the opening sales assumption or the opening price assumption is quite straightforward, involving placing the cursor on the figure and entering the new value. On pressing Enter the spreadsheet is re-evaluated and all cells which refer to the changed values, either directly or indirectly, are updated.

The success of performing even the simplest what-if analysis is dependent on the spreadsheet having been developed with the correct series of relationships. For example, changing the opening sales value in Figure 9.7 would automatically cause the other quarter sales values to recalculate, as well as the revenue, costs and

	A	B	C	D	E	F
1						
2			Written by P.A. Jones			
3			pajones@business.com			
4			0118 999 9999			
5						
6		Qtr 1	Qtr 2	Qtr 3	Qtr 4	Total
7	sales	150	=B7*1.15	=C7*1.15	=D7*1.15	=SUM(B7:E7)
8	price	12.55	12.55	12.55	12.55	
9	revenue	=B7*B8	=C7*C8	=D7*D8	=E7*E8	=SUM(B9:E9)
10	costs	=B7*7.897	=C7*7.897	=D7*7.897	=E7*7.897	=SUM(B10:E10)
11	profit	=B9-B10	=C9-C10	=D9-D10	=E9-E10	=SUM(B11:E11)
12						
13						
14	Report Printed		=NOW()	=NOW()		
15						
16						
17						
18						
19						
20						

STYLE05.XLS

Figure 9.7 Absolute values restricting what-if analysis

profit lines, because they relate, through the cell references in the formulae, either directly or indirectly to the sales value in cell B5.

However, as already mentioned this plan incorporates absolute values in the formulae for sales and costs growth. Furthermore, the price is a fixed value and has been entered once into cell B6 and the value has then been copied into the other periods. This presents problems when what-if analysis is required on any of these factors.

Problems with this spreadsheet

Because no growth in the price is required, the opening value of 12.55 has been copied for the four quarters. Whilst this is fine all the time a price of 12.55 is required, it presents a problem if the price needs to be changed. With this spreadsheet it would be necessary to overwrite the price in the first quarter and then copy the new value for the remaining three quarters. The same applies if the sales growth or the cost factors need to be changed.

Spreadsheet 6: Separating growth and cost factors

To prevent the problems in Spreadsheet 5 from arising, a different approach to the development of the plan needs to be taken.

In the first instance, all growth and cost factors should be represented in a separate area of the spreadsheet – even on a different sheet altogether in the case of a large system with a lot of input.

The factors can then be referenced from within the plan as and when they are required. Figure 9.8 shows the adapted layout for this plan after extracting the sales growth and costs factors.

STYLE06.XLS

	A	B	C	D	E	F	G	H
1		Profit Projection for Widget Division for 20XX					Last updated:	Jan 20XX
2			Written by P.A. Jones					
3			pajones@business.com					
4			0118 999 9999					
5								
6								
7		Qtr 1	Qtr 2	Qtr 3	Qtr 4	Total		
8	sales	150	152	153	155	609		
9	price	12.55	12.61	12.68	12.74			
10	revenue	1883	1911	1940	1969	7703		
11	costs	1125	1136	1148	1159	4569		
12	profit	758	775	792	810	3134		
13								
14								
15	Growth in Sales Volume as %			1.01%				
16	Growth in Price as %			0.5%				
17	Cost per unit of production			7.50				
18								
19	Report Printed	22-Mar-05 13:00:00						
20								
21								
22								

Figure 9.8 Using cell references for non-changing values

Having the growth and cost factors in separate cells means that the formulae need to be changed to pick up this information. Figure 9.9 shows the amended formulae for this plan.

	A	B	C	D	E	F
1			Profit Projection for Widget Division for 20XX			Last
2			Written by P.A. Jones			
3			pajones@business.com			
4			0118 999 9999			
5						
6						
7		Qtr 1	Qtr 2	Qtr 3	Qtr 4	Total
8	sales	150	=B8*(1+$D$15)	=C8*(1+$D$15)	=D8*(1+$D$15)	=SUM(B8:E8)
9	price	12.55	=B9*(1+$D$16)	=C9*(1+$D$16)	=D9*(1+$D$16)	
10	revenue	=B8*B9	=C8*C9	=D8*D9	=E8*E9	=SUM(B10:E10)
11	costs	=B8*$D$17	=C8*$D$17	=D8*$D$17	=E8*$D$17	=SUM(B11:E11)
12	profit	=B10-B11	=C10-C11	=D10-D11	=E10-E11	=SUM(B12:E12)
13						
14						
15	Growth in Sales Volume as %			0.01		
16	Growth in Price as %			0		
17	Cost per unit of production			7.5		
18						
19	Report Printed	=NOW()	=NOW()			
20						
21						

Figure 9.9 Amended formulae to take account of extracted growth and cost factors

Note that the references to cells D15, D16 and D17 are fixed references. This is achieved by placing the $ symbol before the column letter and row number, i.e. $D$15, and means that when the for-mula is copied the reference to cell D15 remains fixed. A shortcut key to add the $ symbols to a cell reference is F4.

In this plan an option in the growth factors has been included for the price, despite the fact that in this plan the price does not change. It is important to always think ahead when developing any plan and although the price does not currently change, it might be necessary to include a percentage increase in the future. Having the facility for change built-in to the plan could save time later – and for the time being the growth factor is simply set to zero.

Removing the growth and cost factors from the main body of a business plan is the first step in developing a data input form which will ultimately separate all the input data from the actual logic of the spreadsheet. This separation of the data allows the logic cells to be protected from accidental damage. This is discussed further in the 'Template' section of this chapter.

Spreadsheet 7: Optimizing layout

The amount of detail supplied in the plan so far is clearly insufficient for any real decision-making process.

More detail of the firm's cost structure would constitute an obvious improvement and Figure 9.10 shows how this might be incorporated. This sample plan is obviously small, and even the expanded plan fits onto a screen, but wherever possible do try and divide plans into sections that fit comfortably in the screen area, and indicate if there is more information to follow by writing in a prompt such as press page down for cost analysis.

Some people might find the spreadsheet in Figure 9.10 disjointed with revenue in one section and the costs in another. Although good spreadsheet design is essential, personal preference will always have a role to play in the finished result, and of course the way in which a system is used and for what purpose will play an important role in deciding which variables are grouped together. For example, it is not difficult to restructure this plan as shown in Figure 9.11.

STYLE07A.XLS

	A	B	C	D	E	F	G	H
1	Profit Projection for Widget Division for 20XX						Last Updated	31 July 20XX
2	Written by P.A. Jones 31 July 20XX							
3	pajones@business.com							
4	0118 999 9999							
5								
6								
7		Qtr 1	Qtr 2	Qtr 3	Qtr 4	Total		
8	Sales volume	2500	2525	2551	2577	10153		
9	Unit price	12.55	12.61	12.68	12.74			
10	Revenue	31375	31850	32333	32823	128381		
11	Costs	22435	22553	22673	22795	90456		
12	**Gross Profit/Loss**	**8940**	**9297**	**9660**	**10028**	**37925**		
13								
14	*Factors*							
15	Growth in sales volume as %	1.01%						
16	Growth in Price as %	0.5%						
17								
18	**Cost Analysis**							
19	Raw Materials	8125	8207	8290	8374	32996		
20	Labour	5000	5000	5000	5000	20000		
21	Energy	1200	1236	1273	1311	5020		
22	Depreciation	110	110	110	110	440		
23	**Total direct costs**	**14435**	**14553**	**14673**	**14795**	**58456**		
24								
25	Overheads	8000	8000	8000	8000	32000		
26								
27	**Total Costs**	**22435**	**22553**	**22673**	**22795**	**90456**		
28								
29	*Cost Factors*							
30	Cost of raw materials	3.25						
31	Labour cost increase	0.00%						
32	Energy cost increase	3.00%						
33								

Figure 9.10 Expanded cost structure

STYLE07B.XLS

	A	B	C	D	E	F	G	H
1	Profit Projection for Widget Division for 20XX						Last Updated	31 July 20XX
2	Written by P.A. Jones 31 July 20XX							
3	pajones@business.com							
4	0118 999 9999							
5								
6								
7		Qtr 1	Qtr 2	Qtr 3	Qtr 4	Total		
8	Sales volume	2500	2525	2551	2577	10153		
9	Unit price	12.55	12.61	12.68	12.74			
10	**Revenue**	**31375**	**31850**	**32333**	**32823**	**128381**		
11								
12	**Costs**							
13	Raw Materials	8125	8207	8290	8374	32996		
14	Labour	5000	5000	5000	5000	20000		
15	Energy	1200	1236	1273	1311	5020		
16	Depreciation	110	110	110	110	440		
17	**Total direct costs**	**14435**	**14553**	**14673**	**14795**	**58456**		
18								
19	Overheads	8000	8000	8000	8000	32000		
20								
21	**Total Costs**	**22435**	**22553**	**22673**	**22795**	**90456**		
22								
23	**Gross Profit/Loss**	**8940**	**9297**	**9660**	**10028**	**37925**		
24								
25	*Factors*							
26	Growth in sales volume as %	1.01%						
27	Growth in Price as %	0.5%						
28	Cost of raw materials	3.25						
29	Labour cost increase	0.00%						
30	Energy cost increase	3.00%						
31								

Figure 9.11 Alternative approach for expanding costs

Spreadsheet 8: Arithmetic cross-checks

As already mentioned spreadsheet users are not inherently good at auditing plans as thoroughly as perhaps they should, and therefore an important aspect of spreadsheet design is to build into the system checks on the arithmetical accuracy that will raise the alarm if things begin to go wrong. This might include validating input data through the use of an IF function, or performing a cross-check on a calculation.

When creating calculation checks the first step is to select a number of key items from the model, whose result can be calculated using a different arithmetic reference. For example, in Figure 9.12 below the year end gross profit has been calculated by referencing the individual total values in column F and then by totalling the values in the gross profit row. An IF function is then applied to compare the two results and if they are not the same the word 'error' is displayed in cell D8.

STYLE08.XLS

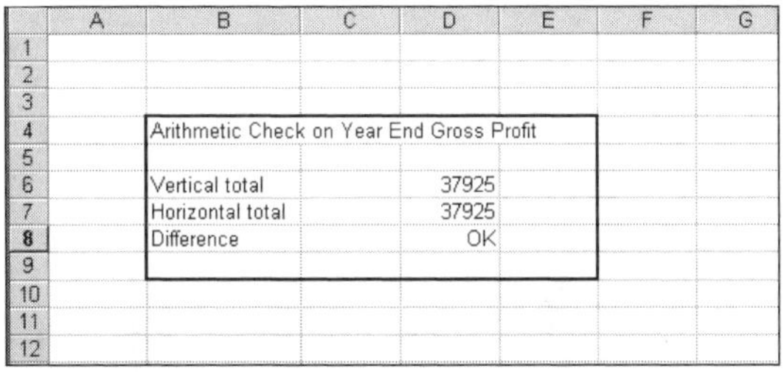

Figure 9.12 Cross-check control box

The formulae required in cells D6 and D7, which calculate the year end gross profit from the plan illustrated in Figure 9.11 are:

For the vertical total

> ='P&L ACCOUNT'!F10−'P&L ACCOUNT'!F17−'P&L ACCOUNT'!F19
> =F10−F17−F19

and for the horizontal total

> =SUM('P&L ACCOUNT'!B23:E24)

The formula in cell D8 is an IF function that compares the two cells as follows:

> =IF(D6<>D7,"ERROR","OK")

A macro could also be created that alerts the user should the arithmetic not balance, probably by a beep and going to a suitable message screen.

Spreadsheet 9: Charts

It is useful to support the information supplied in business plans with charts. In the profit and loss account used in this chapter, various charts might be useful, for example, to show the relative impact of price and sales volume figures. Although charts can be placed on the same worksheet as the plan, it is usually preferable to keep graphs on separate *chart sheets*. The exception might be if it is appropriate to view changes on a chart at the same time data in the plan is changed, or if a spreadsheet is to be copied into a management report being created in Word. Figure 9.13 is an example of the type of chart that might be produced from the plan used in this chapter. This chart has been received using the data in Figure 9.11.

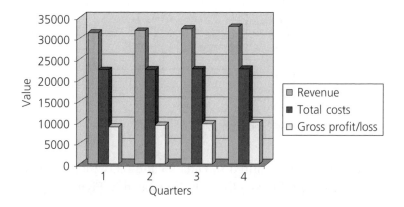

Figure 9.13 Three-dimensional graph

Spreadsheet 10: Mutiple sheets

The plan used in this chapter has been a simple quarterly plan, but in many cases business plans will be larger and more complex. Figure 9.14 is an extract from a five year quarterly plan. Although it is not obvious by looking at Figure 9.14, each year this report has been formatted with a different colour font. This is a useful technique when working with large models because it enables the user to quickly know which part of the plan is being viewed or worked on, without having to scroll around the spreadsheet to see the titles. This colour coding can then be carried over to summary reports, and other reports pertaining to the different parts of the plan.

From a design point of view it is preferable to place different reports associated with a plan on separate worksheets. The report in Figure 9.15, which has been placed on a separate sheet called *Summary* is created by referencing the cells from the yearly totals in the main plan.

To assign a name to a worksheet simply double click on the sheet reference at the bottom of the screen and type in the required name.

TECHNIQUE TIP!

	A	B	C	D	E	F	G	H	I	J	K
1	Five Year Profit Projection for Widget Division for 1998										
2	Written by P.A. Jones 31 July 1997										
3											
4		Y1 Qtr 1	Y1 Qtr 2	Y1 Qtr 3	Y2 Qtr 4	Y1 Total	Y2 Qtr 1	Y2 Qtr 2	Y2 Qtr 3	Y2 Qtr 4	Y2 Total
5	Sales Volume	8000	8080	8161	8242	32483	12000	12000	12000	12000	48000
6	Price	50.00	50.75	51.51	52.28		67.00	67.00	67.00	67.00	
7	Revenue	400000	410060	420373	430945	1661378	804000	804000	804000	804000	3216000
8											
9	Raw Materials	96000	96960	97930	98909	389798	180000	180000	180000	180000	720000
10	Labour	12000	12060	12120	12181	48361	15000	15150	15302	15455	60906
11	Energy	9600	9792	9988	10188	39567	10000	10050	10100	10151	40301
12	Depreciation	2000	2020	2040	2061	8121	2500	2519	2538	2557	10113
13	Total Direct Costs	119600	120832	122078	123338	485848	207500	207719	207939	208162	831320
14											
15	Gross Profit	280400	289228	298295	307607	1175530	596500	596281	596061	595838	2384680
16	Overheads	20000	20300	20605	20914	81818	22000	22220	22442	22667	89329
17											
18	Net Profit	260400	268928	277691	286694	1093712	574500	574061	573618	573171	2295351

STYLE10.XLS

Figure 9.14 Five year extended plan

	A	B	C	D	E	F	G
1	Five Year Summary Profit Projection for Widget Division for 1998						
2	Written by P.A. Jones 31 July 1997						
3							
4		Y1 Total	Y2 Total	Y3 Total	Y4 Total	Y5 Total	5 yr Total
5	Sales Volume	32483	48000	60452	72542	90675	304152
6	Average Annual Price	51.14	67.00	70.97	71.06	71.06	
7	Revenue	1661378	3216000	4290334	5154924	6444709	20767344
8							
9	Raw Materials	389798	720000	1027676	1233211	1813508	5184192
10	Labour	48361	60906	64966	68000	70067	312301
11	Energy	39567	40301	40301	48361	113750	282281
12	Depreciation	8121	10113	10113	12090	12945	53382
13	Total Direct Costs	485848	831320	1143056	1361662	2010270	5832156
14							
15	Gross Profit	1175530	2384680	3147278	3793262	4434439	14935189
16	Overheads	81818	89329	89329	89329	97816	447621
17							
18	Net Profit	1093712	2295351	3057949	3703933	4336623	14487568

Figure 9.15 Summary report

107

Templates

A business plan that requires time and effort to design and implement is likely to be in regular use for some time. In addition, the data in the plan will almost certainly change, either as situations within the business change, or on a periodic basis. In such circumstances it is advisable to convert the developed plan into a template, into which different data can be entered whenever necessary.

A template is a plan that contains the logic required, i.e. the formulae, but from which the data has been removed. When new data is entered the formulae will be calculated. Figure 9.16 shows the simplest approach to creating a template. Taking the one-year quarterly plan used in this chapter the input data and growth factors have been removed and these cells have been highlighted by shading the cells. The file can be found on the CD accompanying the book under the name **TEMPLAT1**.

When the input cells are set to zero all other cells that are directly or indirectly related to those cells should also display zero. The only exception to this is if there are division formulae in which case a division by zero error will be displayed. The act of removing

	A	B	C	D	E	F	G	H
1	Profit Projection for Widget Division for 20XX						Last Updated	31 July 20XX
2	Written by P.A. Jones 31 July 20XX							
3	pajones@business.com							
4	0118 999 9999							
5								
6								
7		Qtr 1	Qtr 2	Qtr 3	Qtr 4	Total		
8	Sales volume		0	0	0	0		
9	Unit price		0.00	0.00	0.00			
10	Revenue	0	0	0	0	0		
11								
12	Costs							
13	Raw Materials	0	0	0	0	0		
14	Labour		0	0	0	0		
15	Energy		0	0	0	0		
16	Depreciation		0	0	0	0		
17	Total direct costs	0	0	0	0	0		
18								
19	Overheads		0	0	0	0		
20								
21	Total Costs	0	0	0	0	0		
22								
23	Gross Profit/Loss	0	0	0	0	0		
24								
25	Factors							
26	Growth in sales volume as %							
27	Growth in Price as %							
28	Cost of raw materials							
29	Labour cost increase							
30	Energy cost increase							
31								
32								

Figure 9.16 Plan converted to a template

the data is in itself a useful auditing tool, because if values are found in any cells this indicates that there is an error in the way that the plan was developed which can be rectified.

When the template is complete the spreadsheet should be protected, specifying only the cells into which data can be entered as unprotected cells. This is a two-step process. First, the cells into which data can be entered are unprotected using the FORMAT CELLS PROTECTION command and removing the tick on the Locked box. The second step is to then enable protection by selecting TOOLS PROTECTION PROTECT SHEET.

It is also important to save the file now as a Template file as opposed to a Worksheet file. This is achieved by selecting FILE SAVE AS Template (*.XLT) in the File Type box. The location of the template file defaults to the directory where other Microsoft Office template files are located. To use the template, File New is selected which accesses the Template directory and when a file is selected a copy of it is opened, leaving the original template unchanged on the disk.

Data input forms

A further enhancement that makes working with templates easier to control is to remove all the data from the main plan and place it on one or more data input forms which will normally be located on separate worksheets. Figure 9.17 is a data input form for the

	A	B	C	D
1	Profit Projection for Widget Division for 20XX			
2	Data Input Form			
3		Opening input	Growth or cost factor	
4	Sales volume	0.00	0.00%	
5	Unit price	0.00	0.00%	
6				
7	**Costs**			
8	Labour	0.00	0.00%	
9	Cost of raw materials	n/a	0.00	
10	Energy	0.00	0.00%	
11	Depreciation	0.00	0.00%	
12				
13	Overheads	0.00	0.00%	
14				
15				
16				

TEMPLAT2.XLS

Figure 9.17 Data input form

	A	B	C	D	E	F
1			Profit Projection for Widget Division for 20XX			Last Update
2			Written by P.A. Jones 31 July 20XX			
3			pajones@business.com			
4			0118 999 9999			
5						
6						
7			Qtr 1	Qtr 2	Qtr 3	Qtr 4	Total
8	Sales volume	=Input form!B4	=B8*(1+Input form!$C$4)	=C8*(1+Input form!$C$4)	=D8*(1+Input form!$C$4)	=SUM(B8:E8)
9	Unit price	=Input form!B5	=B9*(1+Input form!$C$5)	=C9*(1+Input form!$C$5)	=D9*(1+Input form!$C$5)	
10	Revenue	=B8*B9	=C8*C9	=D8*D9	=E8*E9	=SUM(B10:E10)
11						
12	Costs					
13	Labour	=Input form!B8	=B13*(1+Input form!$C$8)	=C13*(1+Input form!$C$8)	=D13*(1+Input form!$C$8)	=SUM(B13:E13)
14	Raw Materials	=B8*Input form!$C$9	=C8*Input form!$C$9	=D8*Input form!$C$9	=E8*Input form!$C$9	=SUM(B14:E14)
15	Energy	=Input form!B10	=B15*(1+Input form!$C$10)	=C15*(1+Input form!$C$10)	=D15*(1+Input form!$C$10)	=SUM(B15:E15)
16	Depreciation	=Input form!B11	=B16*(1+Input form!$C$11)	=C16*(1+Input form!$C$11)	=D16*(1+Input form!$C$11)	=SUM(B16:E16)
17	Total direct costs	=SUM(B13:B16)	=SUM(C13:C16)	=SUM(D13:D16)	=SUM(E13:E16)	=SUM(F14:F16)
18						
19	Overheads	=Input form!B13	=B19*(1+Input form!$C$13)	=C19*(1+Input form!$C$13)	=D19*(1+Input form!$C$13)	=SUM(B19:E19)
20						
21	Total Costs	=B17+B19	=C17+C19	=D17+D19	=E17+E19	=F17+F19
22						
23	Gross Profit/Loss	=B10-B21	=C10-C21	=D10-D21	=E10-E21	=F10-F21
24						

Figure 9.18 Amended formulae to reference data input form

quarterly plan, and Figure 9.18 shows the amended formulae in the plan which picks up the data from the input form.

There are many benefits to be derived from using data input forms including the fact that the data can be checked more easily. Sometimes it might be possible to design an input form that is compatible with a forecasting or accounting system so that the data can be electronically picked up from the other system without having to type it in again. Even if this is not possible, the order of items in the data input form does not have to be the same as the order in which they are referenced in the logic, which means that the data input form can be created to be as compatible with the source of the input data as possible. Furthermore, the worksheet containing the logic for the plan can be protected, and if necessary made read-only, in order to maintain the integrity of the system.

It is not a trivial task to change existing systems to be templates with data input forms, and it will also take a little longer to develop a new system in this way, as opposed to incorporating the data with the logic. However, the ease of data input and ongoing maintenance should make the additional effort worth-while.

Summary

This chapter has considered some of the principal design elements that should be considered when embarking on the creation of any business model or plan, be it a financial statement, a budgetary control system, a marketing model or a forecasting plan. A small plan has been used for demonstration purposes, and many of the techniques illustrated become essential when working with larger plans. Taking time to consider the layout and design of a system before embarking on its development has been proven by many users to pay considerable dividends in the long term. In addition it is worth talking with colleagues who might find a plan useful before starting development to see whether some additional lines should be incorporated, as it is always more difficult to add to a spreadsheet later.

10

Developing a Financial Plan

Planning unifies diverse activities, providing a 'road map' for the undertaking of complete tasks that must be well co-ordinated, accomplished over extended time frames and inclusive of many people.

– R.K. Wysocki and J. Young, Information Systems – Management Principles in Action, 1990.

Introduction

Financial planning is a popular spreadsheet application, which often involves acquiring a sales forecast, perhaps using one of the models or methods described in Part 1 of this book, and then specifying all the resources necessary to ensure that the forecast targets are reached. Financial planning can be performed for an entire organisation, or for a department or division. When separate divisional profit plans are developed they may subsequently be incorporated into a corporate plan.

The model

The financial plan described in this chapter is a one year quarterly plan for a manufacturing company. It is a deterministic plan and assumes point estimates for the opening input values, as well as the growth and cost factors. In this example all growth rates and cost factors remain the same for the duration of the plan. The completed model can be found on the CD accompanying this book under the name FINPLAN.

The plan consists of six separate worksheets. The first is a Data Input sheet. For this example all the input data has been grouped onto one sheet, but in some situations, if there is a large amount of input, it might be preferable to break the input down into multiple sheets. The second worksheet is a Profit and Loss Account that shows how the firms' income will be made and what costs will be incurred in generating this income. The Profit and Loss Appropriation Account, which provides an estimate of tax payable, the dividends payable and the funds to be transferred to reserve accounts for future growth is also on this worksheet.

The third worksheet is a Balance Sheet, followed by Funds Flow Statement, some Ratio Analysis and finally a Cash Flow Statement.

Getting started

The first step when creating a multi-sheet plan such as this is to collect as much information as possible in terms of the line items, variables, growth and cost factors, etc., and then to name worksheets and

	A	B	C	D	E	F
1	**Input Area for all parts**					
2						
3	**Profit and Loss Account**					
4		*Opening Figs*	*Growth*	*Open Prop*	*Base Variable*	
5	Volume	6000	3.00%			
6	Unit Price	10	2.00%			
7	Materials per Unit	4				
8	Labour	10000	1.50%			
9	Energy	8000	2.00%			
10	Administration			2.50%	of turnover	
11	Depreciation	1500				
12	Finance Charges	1200				
13	Maintenance			0.01	per unit	
14	Salaries	13000	6.00%			
15						
16	Corporate Tax Rate	30.00%				
17						
18	**Profit and Loss Appropriation Account**					
19		*1 qtr*	*2 qtr*	*3 qtr*	*4 qtr*	
20	Dividends	0	2100	0	2100	
21	Reserves	0	0	0	3500	
22						
23	**Balance Sheet**					
24	ASSETS					
25	Fixed assets	*Opening Bal*				
26	Land & Building	45000				
27	Plant & Equipment	26500				
28	Fixtures & Fittings	4500				
29	Motor Vehicles	7500				
30	Depreciation	15000				
31						
32	Current assets	*Opening Bal*				
33	Inventory	39500				
34	Debtors	67000				
35	Prepayments	1000				
36	Cash	24000				
37						
38						
39	CAPITAL					
40		*Opening Bal*				
41	Share capital	75000				
42	Retained profit	9250				
43	Reserves	5500				
44						
45	LIABILITIES					
46	Long term liabilities	*Opening Bal*				
47	Debenture	20000				
48	Loan	25250				
49	Mortgage	30500				
50						
51	Current Liabilities	*Opening Bal*				
52	Trade creditors	30500				
53	Tax	2500				
54	Dividends	1500				
55						
56		*Opening Bal*				
57	Previous periods sales	36500				

Figure 10.1 Data Input worksheet (*Input*)

enter titles, column headings and line item descriptions. This forms the basic structure of the plan and makes cross-sheet referencing possible when formulae are developed. Figures 10.1 through 10.6 show the six worksheets that make up the full plan with sample data.

	A	B	C	D	E	F	G
1	**Final Accounts Template**						
2							
3	**Profit & Loss Account**		*1st qtr.*	*2nd qtr.*	*3rd qtr.*	*4th qtr.*	*Total*
4	Volume		6000	6180	6365	6556	25102
5	Unit price		10.00	10.20	10.40	10.61	
6	**Turnover**		60000	63036	66226	69577	258838
7							
8	Materials		24000	24720	25462	26225	100407
9	Labour		10000	10150	10302	10457	40909
10	Energy		8000	8160	8323	8490	32973
11	**Total direct costs**		42000	43030	44087	45172	174289
12							
13	**Gross Profit**		18000	20006	22139	24405	84549
14							
15	Administration		1500	1576	1656	1739	6471
16	Depreciation		1500	1500	1500	1500	6000
17	Finance charges		1200	1200	1200	1200	4800
18	Maintenance		600	630	662	696	2588
19	Salaries		13000	13780	14607	15483	56870
20	**Total other costs**		17800	18686	19625	20618	76729
21							
22	**Net Profit B.T.**		200	1320	2514	3786	7820
23							
24	Provision for tax		60	396	754	1136	2346
25	**Net Profit A.T.**		140	924	1760	2650	5474
26	**Cumulative profit**		140	1064	2824	5474	
27							
28	Dividends		0	2100	0	2100	4200
29	Reserves		0	0	0	3500	3500
30	Cumulative apportionments		0	2100	2100	7700	7700
31	**Retained Profit**		140	-1176	1760	-2950	

Figure 10.2 Profit and Loss Account worksheet (*P&L*)

The worksheets have been named as follows: *Input, P&L, Balsheet, Funds Flow, Ratios* and *Cash Flow*. These names will be referenced by formulae when cross-sheet references are required.

Developing the Profit and Loss Account

The data input sheet in Figure 10.1 shows all the assumptions that have been made for the Profit and Loss Account. For example, the sales volume begins at 6000 and increases by 3% per period, the unit price begins at 10 and increases at 2%, the cost of raw materials is £4 per unit, etc.

Having prepared the structure for this part of the plan the logic can now be entered. The opening sales volume value is required in cell

	A	B	C	D	E	F
1	Balance Sheet at 31 December 2XXX					
2						
3	ASSETS					
4	Fixed assets	Opening Bal	1st qtr.	2nd qtr.	3rd qtr.	4th qtr.
5	Land & Building	45000	45000	45000	45000	45000
6	Plant & Equipment	26500	26500	26500	26500	26500
7	Fixtures & Fittings	4500	4500	4500	4500	4500
8	Motor Vehicles	7500	7500	7500	7500	7500
9	Depreciation	15000	16500	18000	19500	21000
10	Total net fixed assets	68500	67000	65500	64000	62500
11						
12	Current assets	Opening Bal	1st qtr.	2nd qtr.	3rd qtr.	4th qtr.
13	Inventory	39500	39500	39500	39500	39500
14	Debtors	67000	60000	63036	66226	69577
15	Prepayments	1000	1000	1000	1000	1000
16	Cash	24000	37500	38270	40111	43094
17	Total current assets	131500	138000	141806	146836	153170
18						
19	Current Liabilities					
20	Trade creditors	30500	35300	36286	37303	38350
21	Tax	2500	2560	2956	3710	4846
22	Dividends	1500	1500	3600	3600	5700
23	Total Current Liabilities	34500	39360	42842	44613	48896
24						
25	Working Capital	97000	98640	98964	102224	104274
26	Total assets	165500	165640	164464	166224	166774
27						
28	Long term liabilities					
29	Debenture	20000	20000	20000	20000	20000
30	Loan	25250	25250	25250	25250	25250
31	Mortgage	30500	30500	30500	30500	30500
32	Total long term liabilities	75750	75750	75750	75750	75750
33						
34	Total net assets	89750	89890	88714	90474	91024
35						
36	CAPITAL					
37		Opening Bal	1st qtr.	2nd qtr.	3rd qtr.	4th qtr.
38	Share capital	75000	75000	75000	75000	75000
39	Retained profit	9250	9390	8214	9974	7024
40	Reserves	5500	5500	5500	5500	9000
41	Owners equity	89750	89890	88714	90474	91024
42						
43	Total Capital & Liabilities	165500	165640	164464	166224	166774

Figure 10.3 Balance Sheet worksheet (*Balsheet*)

C4 of the *P&L* sheet and therefore a reference to the *Input* sheet, cell B5 is entered as follows:

=INPUT!$B$5

In the second and subsequent periods the sales volume is to grow by the value entered in cell C5 of the *Input* sheet. The following formula is therefore required in cell D4 of the *P&L* sheet:

=C4*(1+INPUT!$C$5)

This formula can then be extrapolated for the remaining two quarters. Note that the use of the absolute reference ensures that the reference to cell C5 in the *Input* sheet remains fixed.

	A	B	C	D	E	F
1	**Funds Flow Statement**					
2						
3	**ASSETS**					
4	**Fixed assets**			*2nd qtr.*	*3rd qtr.*	*4th qtr.*
5	Land & Building			0	0	0
6	Plant & Equipment			0	0	0
7	Fixtures & Fittings			0	0	0
8	Motor Vehicles			0	0	0
9	Depreciation			1500	1500	1500
10	**Total net fixed assets**			-1500	-1500	-1500
11						
12	**Current assets**					
13	Inventory			0	0	0
14	Debtors			3036	3190	3351
15	Prepayments			0	0	0
16	Cash			770	1841	2983
17	**Total current assets**			3806	5030	6334
18						
19	**Current Liabilities**					
20	Trade creditors			986	1016	1048
21	Tax			396	754	1136
22	Dividends			2100	0	2100
23	**Total Current Liabilities**			3482	1771	4284
24						
25	Working Capital			324	3260	2050
26	**Total Assets**			-1176	1760	550
27						
28	**Long term liabilities**					
29	Debenture			0	0	0
30	Loan			0	0	0
31	Mortgage			0	0	0
32	**Total long term liabilities**			0	0	0
33						
34	**Total net assets**			-1176	1760	550
35						
36	**CAPITAL**					
37				*2nd qtr.*	*3rd qtr.*	*4th qtr.*
38	Share capital			0	0	0
39	Retained profit			-1176	1760	-2950
40	Reserves			0	0	3500
41	**Owners equity**			-1176	1760	550
42						
43	**Total Capital & Liabilities**			-1176	1760	550

Figure 10.4 Funds Flow worksheet (*Funds Flow*)

119

The total sales volume in cell G4 of the *P&L* sheet is calculated with the SUM function as follows:

=SUM(C4:F4)

	A	B	C	D	E	F
1	**Ratio Analysis**					
2			*1st qtr.*	*2nd qtr.*	*3rd qtr.*	*4th qtr.*
3	Current ratio		3.51	3.31	3.29	3.13
4	Quick ratio		2.50	2.39	2.41	2.32
5	Equity to debt		0.78	0.75	0.75	0.73
6	Gross profit %		30.00%	31.74%	33.43%	35.08%
7	Net profit %		0.33%	2.09%	3.80%	5.44%
8	Materials to turnover %		40.00%	39.22%	38.45%	37.69%
9	Labour to turnover %		16.67%	16.10%	15.56%	15.03%
10	Energy to turnover %		13.33%	12.94%	12.57%	12.20%
11	Administration to turnover %		2.50%	2.50%	2.50%	2.50%
12	Depreciation to turnover %		2.50%	2.38%	2.26%	2.16%
13	Finance charges to turnover %		2.00%	1.90%	1.81%	1.72%
14	Maintenance to turnover %		1.00%	1.00%	1.00%	1.00%
15	Salaries to turnover %		21.67%	21.86%	22.06%	22.25%
16	Stock turnover		6.08	6.38	6.71	7.05
17	No. of days in inventory		60	57	54	52
18	Asset turnover		1.45	1.53	1.59	1.67
19	Capital output		0.69	0.65	0.63	0.60
20	Net working capital		98640	98964	102224	104274
21	Working capital turnover		2.43	2.55	2.59	2.67
22	No. of days debtors		91	91	91	91
23	No. of days creditors		88	88	88	88
24	Return on investment		0.48%	3.21%	6.05%	9.08%
25	Return on equity		0.62%	4.17%	7.78%	11.65%

Figure 10.5 Ratio Analysis worksheet (*Ratios*)

	A	B	C	D	E	F
1	**Cash flow plan**					
2			*1st qtr.*	*2nd qtr.*	*3rd qtr.*	*4th qtr.*
3	Opening Cash Balance		24000	37500	38270	40111
4						
5	*Cash in*					
6	Sales from previous period		36500	60000	63036	66226
7	Investments		0	0	0	0
8	Other cash receipts		0	0	0	0
9						
10	*Cash out*					
11	Cash expenses		23000	23930	24909	25940
12	Creditors		30500	35300	36286	37303
13	Tax paid		0	0	0	0
14	Dividends paid		0	0	0	0
15	**Balance**		7000	38270	40111	43094
16	**Cum Balance**		7000	45270	85381	128474

Figure 10.6 Cash Flow Statement worksheet (*Cash Flow*)

The remaining lines in the Profit and Loss Account follow the same principles and Figure 10.7 shows the formulae for this part of the financial plan.

	A	B	C	D	E	F	G
3	Profit & Loss Ac		1st qtr.	2nd qtr.	3rd qtr.	4th qtr.	Total
4	Volume		=Input!$B$5	=C4*(1+Input!$C$5)	=D4*(1+Input!$C$5)	=E4*(1+Input!$C$5)	=SUM(C4:F4)
5	Unit price		=Input!$B$6	=C5*(1+Input!$C$6)	=D5*(1+Input!$C$6)	=E5*(1+Input!$C$6)	
6	Turnover		=C4*C5	=D4*D5	=E4*E5	=F4*F5	=SUM(C6:F6)
7							
8	Materials		=C4*Input!$B$7	=D4*Input!$B$7	=E4*Input!$B$7	=F4*Input!$B$7	=SUM(C8:F8)
9	Labour		=Input!$B$8	=C9*(1+Input!$C$8)	=D9*(1+Input!$C$8)	=E9*(1+Input!$C$8)	=SUM(C9:F9)
10	Energy		=Input!$B$9	=C10*(1+Input!$C$9)	=D10*(1+Input!$C$9)	=E10*(1+Input!$C$9)	=SUM(C10:F10)
11	Total direct costs		=SUM(C8:C10)	=SUM(D8:D10)	=SUM(E8:E10)	=SUM(F8:F10)	=SUM(G8:G10)
12							
13	Gross Profit		=C6-C11	=D6-D11	=E6-E11	=F6-F11	=G6-G11
14							
15	Administration		=C6*Input!$D$10	=D6*Input!$D$10	=E6*Input!$D$10	=F6*Input!$D$10	=SUM(C15:F15)
16	Depreciation		=Input!$B$11	=C16	=D16	=E16	=SUM(C16:F16)
17	Finance charges		=Input!$B$12	=C17	=D17	=E17	=SUM(C17:F17)
18	Maintenance		=C6*Input!$D$13	=D6*Input!$D$13	=E6*Input!$D$13	=F6*Input!$D$13	=SUM(C18:F18)
19	Salaries		=Input!$B$14	=C19*(1+Input!$C$14)	=D19*(1+Input!$C$14)	=E19*(1+Input!$C$14)	=SUM(C19:F19)
20	Total other costs		=SUM(C15:C19)	=SUM(D15:D19)	=SUM(E15:E19)	=SUM(F15:F19)	=SUM(G15:G19)
21							
22	Net Profit B.T.		=C13-C20	=D13-D20	=E13-E20	=F13-F20	=G13-G20
23							
24	Provision for tax		=C22*Input!$B$16	=D22*Input!$B$16	=E22*Input!$B$16	=F22*Input!$B$16	=SUM(C24:F24)
25	Net Profit A.T.		=C22-C24	=D22-D24	=E22-E24	=F22-F24	=SUM(C25:F25)
26	Cumulative profit		=C25+B26	=D25+C26	=E25+D26	=F25+E26	

Figure 10.7 Formulae for Profit and Loss Account

Developing the Profit and Loss Appropriation Account

The assumptions for the profit and loss appropriation account are again entered on the *Input* sheet and they involve the dividends and reserves. As these values can change for each period, the lines on the *Input* sheet have allowed for four different values to be entered. In this example, dividends of 2100 have been entered in the 2nd and 4th quarters and reserves of 3500 have been entered in the 4th quarter.

The lines in the Appropriation Account on the *P&L* sheet need to refer to the appropriate cells on the *Input* sheet. Figure 10.8 shows the formulae required for this part of the financial plan.

	A	B	C	D	E	F	G
26	Cumulative profit		=C25+B26	=D25+C26	=E25+D26	=F25+E26	
27							
28	Dividends		=Input!B20	=Input!C20	=Input!D20	=Input!E20	=SUM(C28:F28)
29	Reserves		=Input!B21	=Input!C21	=Input!D21	=Input!E21	=SUM(C29:F29)
30	Cumulative apportionments		=C28+C29	=C30+D28+D29	=D30+E28+E29	=E30+F28+F29	=F30
31	Retained Profit		=C26-C30	=D26-D28-D29	=E26-E28-E29	=F26-F28-F29	
32							

Figure 10.8 Formulae for P&L Appropriation Account

Developing the balance sheet

The balance sheet has been developed following the North–South convention, which means that the assets and liabilities are placed in what amounts to a vertical column. This is the more usual convention today with the more traditional, or old-fashioned East–West convention, where the assets and liabilities are placed side by side, being much less frequently used.

Assets

The opening balances and the assumptions with regard to debtors and creditors are again found on the *Input* sheet. The assumptions made for the debtors and creditors in the balance sheet are that they are paid in full in the following period. The only cash payments made are the labour and salary costs.

The fixed assets and the current assets are taken from the *Input* sheet and do not change over the four quarters of the Balance Sheet. The Depreciation in the first quarter is calculated by multiplying the opening balance by the Depreciation value for the first quarter in the *P&L* sheet. This formula can then be copied for the remaining periods.

The debtors are calculated by taking the turnover for the current period.

The logic for the cash calculation in the first quarter is as follows:

(Opening cash balance − Labour − Salaries) + Previous periods' sales)

Therefore, the formula required in cell C16 of the *Balsheet* sheet is:

=(B16−'P&L'!C9−'P&L'!C19)+INPUT!B57

Unfortunately it is not possible to simply extrapolate this formula for the remaining quarters because in the second quarter it is necessary to incorporate the turnover for the first quarter less the trade creditors. Therefore the formula required in cell D16 is:

=(C16−'P&L'!D9−'P&L'!D19)+'P&L'!C6−C20

The formula in cell D16 can then be copied to the fourth quarter in cell F16.

Capital and liabilities

The current liabilities consist of the trade creditors, tax and dividends. The opening balance for the trade creditors is taken from the *Input* sheet, but in the first quarter the creditors are calculated by taking the total direct costs less the labour (which is paid in cash) plus the total other costs less the salaries and depreciation. Therefore the formula required in cell C20, which can be copied for the remaining periods is:

$$=\text{'P\&L'!C11}-\text{'P\&L'!C9}+\text{'P\&L'!C20}-\text{'P\&L'!C19}-\text{'P\&L'!C16}$$

The opening tax and the dividends are both taken from the *Input* sheet and in the first quarter the opening values are added to the provision for tax made and the dividends respectively in the profit and loss account. Therefore the formulae required in cells C20 and C21, which can be copied for the remaining periods are:

$$=\text{B21}+\text{'P\&L'!C24}$$

and

$$=\text{B22}+\text{'P\&L'!C28}$$

The working capital is the total current assets less the total current liabilities and therefore the formula required in cell B25, which can be copied for the remaining periods is:

$$=\text{B17}-\text{B23}$$

The long-term liabilities consist of debenture, loan and mortgage payments, which are all taken from the *Input* sheet and remain the same for the year.

The total net assets are the total assets less the total long-term liabilities and therefore the formula required in cell B34, which can be copied for the remaining periods is:

$$=\text{B26}-\text{B32}$$

Capital consists of share capital, retained profit and reserves. Share capital is taken from the *Input* sheet and carried across for the four quarters. The opening retained profit is also taken from the *Input* sheet, but in the first quarter the retained profit from the first quarter of the profit and loss account is included. Therefore the formula required in cell C39, which can be copied for the remaining periods is:

=B39+'P&L'!C31

The same procedure is required for the reserves by picking up the opening reserves from the balance sheet section of the *Input* sheet and then adding in the reserves from the profit and loss account in the subsequent quarters.

The total capital and liabilities can then be calculated by adding together the total net assets and the owners' equity. Therefore the formula required in cell B43, which can be copied for the remaining periods is:

=B41+B32

Funds flow statement

The funds flow statement is a tool for understanding how funds are being used in the organisation. It indicates into which assets money is being invested or disinvested as well as showing how these funds have been financed or which sources of finance are being repaid.

The statement of source and application of funds is calculated by subtracting two consecutive balance sheets from each other. This will then indicate which assets are increasing or decreasing, and which sources of funds are being used or being paid back.

The layout of a funds flow statement differs from country to country and company to company, and the following shows the principles of how to set up a statement, but readers will need to format the final report to suit individual requirements.

The basic statement can be quickly created on the spreadsheet by copying the headings and titles from the balance sheet (*Balsheet*) onto the *Funds Flow* sheet. The first column of the source and application of funds statement will represent the second quarter, being the first quarter values from the balance sheet less the opening balance, and thus the titles for the opening balance and the first quarter can be deleted. The following formula can then be entered into cell D5:

=BALSHEET!D5−BALSHEET!C5

This formula can be copied for all the remaining cells in the statement.

Ratio analysis

There are many different ratios that can be applied to a financial statement and Figure 10.5 provides a selection that has been calculated on the *Ratios* sheet. Figure 10.9 shows the formulae for the first quarter ratios which have been copied for the remaining periods.

	A	B	C
1	**Ratio Analysis**		
2			*1st qtr.*
3	Current ratio		=BalSheet!C17/BalSheet!C23
4	Quick ratio		=SUM(BalSheet!C14:C16)/BalSheet!C23
5	Equity to debt		=BalSheet!C41/(BalSheet!C32+BalSheet!C23)
6	Gross profit %		='P&L'!C13/'P&L'!C6
7	Net profit %		='P&L'!C22/'P&L'!C6
8	Materials to turnover %		='P&L'!C8/'P&L'!C6
9	Labour to turnover %		='P&L'!C9/'P&L'!C6
10	Energy to turnover %		='P&L'!C10/'P&L'!C6
11	Administration to turnover %		='P&L'!C15/'P&L'!C6
12	Depreciation to turnover %		='P&L'!C16/'P&L'!C6
13	Finance charges to turnover %		='P&L'!C17/'P&L'!C6
14	Maintenance to turnover %		='P&L'!C18/'P&L'!C6
15	Salaries to turnover %		='P&L'!C19/'P&L'!C6
16	Stock turnover		='P&L'!C6/BalSheet!C13*4
17	No. of days in inventory		=BalSheet!C13/('P&L'!C6*4)*365
18	Asset turnover		='P&L'!C6/BalSheet!C26*4
19	Capital output		=1/C18
20	Net working capital		=BalSheet!C17-BalSheet!C23
21	Working capital turnover		='P&L'!C6/Ratios!C20*4
22	No. of days debtors		=BalSheet!C14/('P&L'!C6*4)*365
23	No. of days creditors		=('P&L'!C8+'P&L'!C10+'P&L'!C15+'P&L'!C18)/BalSheet!C20*365/4
24	Return on investment		='P&L'!C22/BalSheet!C26*4
25	Return on equity		='P&L'!C25/BalSheet!C41*4

Figure 10.9 Formulae for ratio analysis

Cash flow statement

Traditional financial statements produced by an organisation are essentially historic in nature. They show what assets have been acquired and how they have been funded, as well as showing what income has been made and how it has been dispersed. Although all this information is considerable value to management, it does suffer from this strong historical perspective. To counter this, organisations developed techniques of forecasting, planning and budgeting and one of the most important tools available to management is the cash flow plan.

The cash flow plan shows what money the organisation expects to receive and from what sources as well as how it intends to spend it.

The cash balance row of the cash flow plan is the same as the cash row of the balance sheet and therefore the formula in cell C3 that is copied for the remaining periods is:

=BALSHEET!B16

The cash-in section includes sales, investments and cash receipts. In this example there are no investments to be considered and no payments are received in cash, but the sales are the turnover from the previous period. Therefore the opening sales figure is a reference to the opening sales in the *Input* sheet:

=INPUT!B57

In the following period the sales from the profit and loss account in cell C6 can be referenced and this can then be copied for the remaining periods.

The cash-out section of the cash flow plan includes the cash expenses, the creditors and repayments. The cash expenses include labour and salaries which means the following formula is required in cell C11 and can be copied for the remaining periods.

='P&L'!C9+'P&L'!C19

The opening creditors in cell C12 can be picked up from Cell B20 in the balance sheet and the reference can be copied for the remaining periods.

There are no tax or dividend payments, although accommodation for these has been included in the cash flow plan. The cash balance can finally be calculated by taking the opening cash balance, adding the total cash in and subtracting the total cash out. Therefore the formula required in cell C15, which can be copied for the remaining periods is:

=C3+SUM(C6:C8)−SUM(C11:C14)

Summary

Having spent a considerable amount of time and effort developing an integrated financial statement such as the one described here, it is likely that it will be used periodically with different data. Because the input has been held separately on the *Input* sheet it is not difficult to convert this plan into a template. This involves removing all the data in the *Input* sheet, or entering zeros into the cells, which will cause the formulae in the other worksheets to return zero results (with the exception of the *Ratios* sheet which will return division by zero errors). The file can then be saved as an .XLT template file. The section on templates in Chapter 9 gives more details on how to do this.

Business Plans

A plan . . . is 'tangible evidence of the thinking of management.' It results from planning.

– J.O. McKinsey quoted by G.A. Steiner in *Top Management Planning,* Macmillan, 1969.

Introduction

This chapter consists of a selection of different business plans that illustrate a range of spreadsheet techniques which readers may find helpful when developing their own systems. The business applications that have been selected for discussion in this chapter represent only a small number of the possible business spreadsheet applications and the areas chosen are:

◆ capital investment appraisal (CIA)
◆ break-even point analysis
◆ learning curve costing
◆ economic order quantity
◆ sales campaign analysis.

For each of these examples the spreadsheet development approach and the key formulae are explained in detail in this chapter. However, it is strongly recommended that readers study these plans in conjunction with the accompanying CD.

Capital investment appraisal

The CIA model described in this chapter uses both discounted and non-discounted techniques.

Discounted techniques are based on the time value of money. By this it is meant that cash received today is more valuable than cash received at future dates. The rationale of this assertion is that cash can be invested as soon as it is received and thus immediately begin earning a return. Therefore, the longer it takes to receive a sum of money, the less value that sum represents in today's terms.

Discounting techniques for CIA reduce amounts paid and received in the future to the equivalent amount paid and received today.

This is achieved through the application of the following formula that is multiplied by the sum of money concerned:

$1/((1+I)^n)$

where I = discount rate and n = number of periods in the future.

There are several *Discounted Cash Flow* (DCF) measures available in the spreadsheet, with the *Net Present Value* (NPV), the *Profitability Index* (PI) and the *Internal Rate of Return* (IRR) being some of the more frequently used.

The CIA plan shown here calculates the NPV and the PI for both a fixed discount rate (FDR) and for a variable or inflation adjusted discount rate (VDR). Non-discounted cash flow measures of pay-back and rate of return are also produced.

The results of the FDR and VDR calculations are presented in such a way that the investment measures dependent on a discount rate can be compared and the difference between a fixed and a variable discount rate on the NPV and PI can be evaluated. The model can be found on the CD accompanying this book under the name CIA.

Net present value

The purpose of the NPV is to calculate the balance between the *trade-off* in investment outlays and *future benefits* in terms of time-adjusted present monetary values. Thus the formula for NPV is:

NPV = present value of cash flow in − present value of investment

NPV is a straightforward way of establishing whether, during the economic life of a project, a minimum earnings standard can be obtained.

The NPV may be defined as the difference between the sum of the values of the cash-in flows, discounted at an appropriate cost of capital, and the present value of the original investment. Provided the NPV is greater than or equal to zero, the investment will earn the firm's required rate of return. The size of the NPV may be considered as either a measure of the surplus which the investment makes over its required return, or as the margin of error which may be made in the estimate of the investment amount before the investment will be rejected.

The interpretation of the NPV should be based on the following rules:

- ◆ If NPV ≥ 0 then invest
- ◆ If NPV < 0 then do not invest.

Profitability index

The PI is defined as the sum of the present values of the cash-in flows divided by the present value of the investment. This produces a rate of return expressed as the number of discounted pounds and pence, or dollars and cents, or any other currency that the investment will earn for every unit of currency originally invested. The formula for the PI is:

$$PI = \frac{\Sigma \text{ Present value of benefits}}{\text{Present value of investment}}$$

Internal rate of return

The IRR is the rate of interest which will cause the NPV to be zero. It is the internally generated return that the investment will earn throughout its life. It is also sometimes referred to as the *yield* of the investment. The formula for the IRR is:

IRR = i, such that NPV = 0

The IRR is the most complex of the three discounted cash-flow statistical measures described here and it needs to be used with care. The IRR may produce incorrect results if the investment shows negative cash flows after the first year of the project.

Developing a capital investment appraisal plan

Figure 11.1 shows the completed CIA plan with some sample data.

CIA.XLS

The investment reports

The investment reports consist of the simple payback and discounted payback in years and months, the rate of return, the NPV, the PI and the IRR at a fixed discount rate, as well as the payback, NPV and the PI at a variable discount rate.

	A	B	C	D	E	F	G
1	**Capital Investment Appraisal System**						
2			Cash-Out	Cash-In	Net Cash	Movement each year	
3	IT Investment - Cash Out		350000			-350000	
4	Net Benefits	Year 1		60000		60000	
5		Year 2		95000		95000	
6		Year 3		120000		120000	
7		Year 4		180000		180000	
8		Year 5		200000		200000	
9	Fixed Cost of Capital or Interest Rate	20.00%					
10		Y1	Y2	Y3	Y4	Y5	
11	Estimated inflation rates	3.00%	4.00%	4.00%	3.00%	2.00%	
12							
13	Investment Reports for proposed investment						
14	Payback in years & months	3	years		5	months	
15	Discounted Payback FDR in years & months	4	years		11	months	
16	Rate of return(%)	37.43%					
17	NPV Fixed Discount Rate (FDR)	2598					
18	Profitability Index FDR (PI)	1.01					
19	Internal Rate of Return (IRR)	20.28%					
20							
21	Variable Discount Rates						
22	NPV Variable Discount Rates (VDR)	-115523					
23	Profitability Index VDR (PI)	0.67					

Figure 11.1 Capital investment appraisal plan

Some of these reports can be calculated using built-in spreadsheet functions, but others, such as the payback and the variable discount rate reports, require some additional calculations that have been grouped together in a separate area of the spreadsheet. Figure 11.2 shows the work area for the payback calculations.

	A	B	C	D	E	F	G
25	**Payback work area**						
26	Year no.	1	2	3	4	5	
27	Incomes	60000	95000	120000	180000	200000	
28	Cum Cash	60000	155000	275000	455000	655000	
29	Year no.	1	2	3	4	5	
30							
31	Amount after		3	years	275000		
32	Amount remaining				75000		
33	Value payable in following year				180000		
34	Part of year for remaining amount				5	months	
35							
36	Discounted payback work area						
37	Fixed Rate of Interest	20.00%					
38	Year no.	1	2	3	4	5	
39	Cash-Flow	60000	95000	120000	180000	200000	
40	DCF of cash-in	50000	65972	69444	86806	80376	
41	Cumulative DCF	50000	115972	185417	272222	352598	
42	Year no.	1	2	3	4	5	
43							
44	Amount after		4	years	272222		
45	Amount remaining				77778		
46	Value payable in following year				80376		
47	Part of year for remaining amount				11	months	

Figure 11.2 Payback work areas

Simple payback

The simple payback refers to the amount of time it takes for the original investment to be paid back in nominal terms.

Rows 26 through 29 is a lookup table from which the data for the simple payback is derived. The reason for repeating the year numbers will become clear shortly, but it is to do with how the HLOOKUP function operates.

The formulae in the range B31 through D34 could be combined into a single, nested formula. However, it is preferable to avoid long complex formulae and to break an operation down into a number of smaller modules. This makes auditing and amending the formula much easier.

The first step in calculating the payback is to ascertain the year in which the payback occurs in cell B31. The HLOOKUP function is used. This function requires three pieces of information.

1. What is to be looked up. In this case it is the amount invested in cell C3.
2. The location of the lookup table, which is B28 through F29. The system will then look for the value in C3 across the first row of the specified table range. If an exact match cannot be found it will pick up the next lowest value. For this function to work properly in this context, it is necessary for the values in the first row of the table to be sorted in ascending order.
3. The number of rows to count down for the result, where the first row of the table is 1.

The following is the formula required for cell B31.

=HLOOKUP(C3,B28:F29,2)

Given the data in the plan this formula will lookup 350,000 in the first row of the table range B28 through F29 and, not finding an exact match, will find 275,000 as the next lowest, coming down 1 row in the table will return 3 as the result. In other words, payback is received in year 3.

In order to ascertain which month in year 3 payback occurs, it is necessary to know the funds received by the beginning of year 3. The following formula is required in cell D31:

=HLOOKUP(B31,B26:F28,3)

This formula looks up the value 3 in the table range B26 through F28 and then returns the value 2 rows down, which is 275,000.

The amount of money outstanding is calculated in cell D32 by subtracting the value in cell D31 from the investment in cell C3 which in this example is 75,000.

To be able to calculate what proportion of a year this represents, the amount of cash due in year 4 must be calculated as follows:

=HLOOKUP(B31+1,B26:F29,2)

This produces a result of 180,000. The number of months can then be calculated by dividing 75,000 by 180,000 and multiplying by 12 in cell D34 as follows:

=D32/D33*12

Cell B14 in the main investment report area is simply a reference to cell B32 in the work area and cell D14 is a reference to cell D34 in the work area.

The calculation of the payback is a good example of when a substantial amount of work is required to calculate something that can be visually calculated quite easily just by looking at the data on the screen. However, to ensure that an up-to-date payback is always reported the logic must be built-in to the plan.

Discounted payback

The simple payback as described above is not regarded as being an adequate measure of investment performance because it does not take into account the time value of money. The discounted payback, which is calculated after the future cash flows have been discounted, is regarded as a much stronger indication of the realistic period required to recover the investment. This calculation requires each cash flow to be individually discounted and the new discounted values are then used in the same way as was shown in the simple payback. The formula required for the discounted cash flow in row 40 of Figure 11.2 is as follows:

=B39/(1+$B$37)^B38

As with the simple payback cells B15 and D15 are references to cells B45 and D48 in the work area.

Rate of return

The rate of return is calculated by taking the average of the cash-in flows and dividing by the original investment, expressed as a percentage. Thus the following formula is required in cell B16:

=AVERAGE(D4:D8)/C3

NPV at a fixed discount rate

The NPV function is used to calculate the net present value. This function requires reference to the discount rate and the cash-in flows. The following formula is required in cell B17:

=NPV(B9,D4:D8)−C3

Note that it is necessary to subtract the original investment outside of the NPV function.

Profitability index (PI)

The PI also uses the NPV function, but the result is divided by the original investment as can be seen in the formula in cell B18:

=NPV(B9,D4:D8)/C3

Internal rate of return

The IRR function is used to calculate the IRR in cell B19. This function requires reference to cash-in flows, but the first cell in the range must be the original investment expressed as a negative value. Furthermore, after specifying the data range the function requires a 'guess'. Thus the formula for cell B19 is:

=IRR(F3:F8,0.3)

Note that the original investment and cash-in flows were copied into column F, with the investment represented as a negative value and it is this range that has been used for the IRR calculation.

A 'guess' is entered for the IRR because the calculation of the IRR is a reiterative process and the system requires a 'seed' from which to base the calculation. If no guess is entered the system will assume

0.1 or 10% and this is usually sufficient for a result to be calculated within 0.00001%. If IRR cannot find a result that works after 20 tries, the #NUM! error value is returned.

If IRR gives the #NUM! error value, or if the result is not close to what you expected, try again with a different value for guess.

NPV and PI at variable discount rate

A separate work area is required to be able to calculate the NPV using a discount rate that varies from year to year. Figure 11.3 shows the work area required.

	A	B	C	D	E	F
49	Variable discount rate work area					
50	Year no.	1	2	3	4	5
51	Cash-Flow	60000	95000	120000	180000	200000
52	Discounted 1 period	48780	76613	96774	146341	163934
53	Discounted 2 periods	62287	61785	78044	118977	
54	Discounted 3 periods	50231	49826	62938		
55	Discounted 4 periods	40509	40182			
56	Discounted 5 periods	32669				
57						
58	Sum of Present Values	234477				
59	Net Present Value	-115523				
60	Profitability Index	0.67				

Figure 11.3 Variable discount rate work area

The NPV function assumes a constant rate of interest over the duration of the investment and therefore to accommodate an interest or discount rate that can change each year, the PV function needs to be used. In this context, the PV function is used one year at a time and the discounted value is picked up year by year by a new PV function which adjusts it appropriately. In the example, the cash-in flows have to be discounted over the five years.

In cells B51 to F51 the nominal cash-flow amounts are discounted for one year using the following formula:

=PV(B$11 + $B$9,1,−B50)

Note that the PV function assumes that the cash-flow value is negative (i.e. a credit) and in the above formula this has been reversed by the negative reference to B50. The reference to B11 has the row fixed with the $ which means that the formula can be copied holding the reference to row 11 absolute but changing the column reference. Figure 11.4 shows the formulae in the first two columns.

	A	B	C
48			
49	Variable discount rate v		
50	Year no.	1	2
51	Cash-Flow	=D4	=D5
52	Discounted 1 period	=PV(B$11+$B$9,1,-B51)	=PV(C$11+$B$9,1,-C51)
53	Discounted 2 periods	=PV(B$11+B9,1,-C52)	=PV(C$11+$B$9,1,-C52)
54	Discounted 3 periods	=PV(B$11+$B$9,1,-C53)	=PV(C$11+$B$9,1,-C53)
55	Discounted 4 periods	=PV(B$11+$B$9,1,-C54)	=PV(C$11+$B$9,1,-C54)
56	Discounted 5 periods	=PV(B$11+$B$9,1,-C55)	
57			
58	Sum of Present Values	=SUM(B52:B56)	
59	Net Present Value	=B58-C3	
60	Profitability Index	=B58/C3	

Figure 11.4 Formulae for calculating NPV at a variable discount rate

In rows 52 and 55 each future cash flow from year 2 to 5 is again discounted using a unique interest rate for each year until the cash flow in year 5 has been discounted five times and the cash flow in year has been discounted four times, etc. The individual cash streams are then summed and in the usual way the investment is subtracted from this amount to produce the net present value.

There are clearly other financial reports that could be calculated from this capital investment plan, but those discussed here are intended to give the reader some exposure to some of the more frequently encountered issues.

Learning curve costing

The learning curve costing model is a deterministic plan that demonstrates how unit cost of production will vary as a result of improvements in the production process. The underlying assumption of this model is that the efficiency of labour and material utilisation will improve as the organisation learns from its experience in the manufacture of the product. Thus, unit costs will decrease as improvements in labour efficiency and material usage are effected. The model is on the CD accompanying this book under the name LEARN.

Developing the plan

The plan commences with a data input form in which all the key variables are specified. The first year production figure is required that can be held constant over time in order to see the effect of the improvements in material and labour. Alternatively, the production figure can be increased in order to demonstrate the total effect of an increase in the scale of production, as well as improvements in efficiency.

The input data required for the plan are the first year's production, material costs per unit, labour cost per unit, fixed costs, annual growth production, learning curve effect for materials and labour and the price. The horizon for this plan has been set to 10 years.

The learning curve effect for materials is the percentage improvement in the use of materials that can be achieved per annum over the life of the project. This figure should also include improvement that the firm may achieve through a better buying policy, either due to eventual economies of scale or from finding less expensive sources of the materials. The learning curve effect for labour includes increases in efficiency due to better skills, a higher degree of automation, as well as improved internal procedures. Figure 11.5 shows the plan with some sample data.

	A	B	C	D	E	F	G	H	I
1	Learning Curve Costing over 10 Years								
2									
3	First year's production	2500							
4	Material costs per unit	35.25							
5	Labour costs per unit	25.50							
6	Fixed costs	75000							
7	Annual growth in production	0.00%							
8	Learning curve effect - Materials	5.00%							
9	Learning curve effect - Labour	15.00%							
10	Price	99.99							
11									
12		Year no.	Production	F.Costs	Var.Costs	Unit cost	Revenue		Profit Improvemen
13		1	2500	75000	151875	90.75	249975	23100	0
14		2	2500	75000	137906	85.16	249975	37069	6.56%
15		3	2500	75000	125592	80.24	249975	49383	6.14%
16		4	2500	75000	114707	75.88	249975	60268	5.74%
17		5	2500	75000	105056	72.02	249975	69919	5.36%
18		6	2500	75000	96476	68.59	249975	78499	5.00%
19		7	2500	75000	88823	65.53	249975	86152	4.67%
20		8	2500	75000	81978	62.79	249975	92997	4.36%
21		9	2500	75000	75835	60.33	249975	99140	4.07%
22		10	2500	75000	70306	58.12	249975	104669	3.80%

Figure 11.5 Learning curve costing model

The sample data used in Figure 11.5 has no annual growth rate in production. The effect of this is to highlight the impact on the profit of the learning curve effect alone. If a growth rate in production is specified then the overall profit improvement would be even more dramatic. Therefore a formula is entered into cell C14 and copied for the remaining years to accommodate a possible growth in production which is:

=C13*(1+$B$7)

The formula for the variable costs in column E begins in year 1 by adding the material costs and labour costs and multiplying by the production. Thus the formula in cell E13 is:

=($B$4+$B$5)*C13

In year 2 the learning curve effect for materials and labour is taken into consideration when calculating the variable costs, and therefore the formula in cell E14, which can be copied for the remaining years is:

=($B$4*(1−$B$8)^B13+$B$5*(1−$B$9)^B13)*C14

The unit cost is calculated by adding the fixed and variable costs, and dividing by the production. Thus the formula in cell F13, which can be copied for the remaining years is:

=(D13+E13)/C13

The revenue is the price multiplied by the production and therefore the formula in cell F13, which can be copied for the remaining years is:

=C13*$B$10

The profit is the revenue less the production multiplied by the unit cost and therefore the formula in cell G13, which can be copied for the remaining years is:

=G13−(F13*C13)

Finally, the profit improvement percentage is calculated in column H. Clearly, no improvement can be produced in year 1 and so a zero is entered into cell H13. In year 2 the improvement percentage is calculated by subtracting the profit in the previous year from the profit in the current year and dividing by the total costs. Therefore the formula required in cell H14, which can be copied for the remaining years is:

=(H14−H13)/(D14+E14)

The cumulative effect of the learning curve can be seen not only by the percentage profit improvement, but also by the reduction in unit costs. The chart in Figure 11.6 illustrates this well.

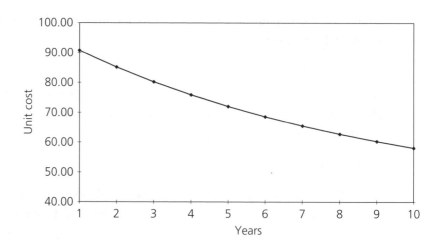

Figure 11.6 Learning curve costing chart

Break-even analysis

The break-even analysis model is a deterministic plan that calculates the volume at which the total costs are equal to the total revenue. The model is on the CD accompanying this book under the name BREAKEVEN. This level of volume is defined as the *break-even* point. The break-even point is derived by calculating the contribution per unit sold, which in turn is defined as the unit selling price less the unit variable cost. The unit contribution is then divided into the fixed costs and the result is the number of units that must be sold for the contribution to absorb the total fixed costs.

The break-even point is not a stationary concept. The volume required in order to pay the total cost continually changes over time due to changes in various costs and prices.

The plan shown here is designed to demonstrate the effect of inflation on the break-even point, which is achieved by providing a growth factor for the fixed costs, the variable costs and the price. When these figures have been entered the break-even point will automatically be extrapolated for four years.

The completed model is shown in Figure 11.7.

	A	B	C	D	E
1	Break-even analysis on Volume				
2					
3		YEAR 1	YEAR 2	YEAR 3	YEAR 4
4	Fixed Costs	6750	7425	8168	8984
5	Variable Costs	34.66	36.39	38.21	40.12
6	Selling Price	98.12	100.57	103.09	105.66
7					
8	Growth in Fixed Costs	10.00%			
9	Growth in Variable Costs	5.00%			
10	Growth in Selling Price	2.50%			
11					
12	Contribution	63.46	64.18	64.87	65.54
13					
14	Break-even unit production	106	116	126	137

Figure 11.7 Break-even point analysis

The formulae required to calculate the break-even point for the plan in Figure 11.7 are not complex and are shown in Figure 11.8.

	A	B	C	D	E
1	Break-even analysis on V				
2					
3		YEAR 1	YEAR 2	YEAR 3	YEAR 4
4	Fixed Costs	6750	=B4*(1+$B$8)	=C4*(1+$B$8)	=D4*(1+$B$8)
5	Variable Costs	34.66	=B5*(1+$B$9)	=C5*(1+$B$9)	=D5*(1+$B$9)
6	Selling Price	98.12	=B6*(1+$B$10)	=C6*(1+$B$10)	=D6*(1+$B$10)
7					
8	Growth in Fixed Costs	0.1			
9	Growth in Variable Costs	0.05			
10	Growth in Selling Price	0.025			
11					
12	Contribution	=B6-B5	=C6-C5	=D6-D5	=E6-E5
13					
14	Break-even unit production	=B4/B12	=C4/C12	=D4/D12	=E4/E12

Figure 11.8 Formulae for break-even analysis

The break-even analysis shown here assumes a single-product situation and frequently this is not the case. Where multiple products are involved the fixed costs or overheads must first be apportioned and then a break-even point calculated for each product or product category. The result will be a break-even point statement for the firm as a whole, which will include a series of volumes, one for each product.

Economic order quantities (EOQ)

There are a range of mathematical techniques available to assist with most aspects of production management, and particularly with the management and control of stock or inventory levels.

The EOQ model calculates the most efficient lot size in which inventory should be purchased. It is a production management technique that is used in many firms. The model is on the CD accompanying the book under the name EOQ.

This is an optimising model which is based on the assumption that the larger the order placed the lower the costs of ordering will be. At the same time, the larger the order placed the higher the carrying costs of stock will be. The EOQ model calculates an optimal level between these two conflicting cost curves.

The input required for the EOQ model are the annual usage in units (AUU), the unit price (UP), the variable cost per order (VCO) and the holding costs as a percentage (HC%). The formula for determining the EOQ is:

$$EOQ = \sqrt{(2 * AUU * VCO / UP * HC\%)}$$

In addition to indicating the lot size, this model is also used to evaluate a supplier's special offer to see whether or not it is worthwhile to purchase in volume in order to obtain a discount.

Developing the EOQ plan

The plan considers three scenarios. The first is the EOQ with no supplier discount policy, the second calculates the EOQ with a supplier discount policy and the third brings in some additional assumptions to calculate the EOQ with lead times and safety stock. Figure 11.9 shows the completed plan.

EOQ.XLS

EOQ with no supplier policy

The required input for calculating the EOQ with no supplier policy is the annual usage in units, the unit price, the holding

	A	B	C	D	E	F	G
1	ECONOMIC ORDER QUANTITY						
2		No Supplier policy	With Supplier policy		With lead times and safety stock		
3	Annual Usage in Units	1250	1250		Annual Usage in Units	1250	
4	Unit Price	60	48		Weekly Usage	24	
5	Variable Cost per Order	28	28		Unit Price	60	
6	Holding Cost as %	30%	30%		Variable Cost per Order	28	
7	Minimum Order		1250		Holding Cost as %	0	
8	EOQ	62	1250		Lead Time in Weeks	8	Assumption
9					Re-order Point	192	
10	Total Cost of Inventory				Possible Delivery Delay in Weeks	3	Assumption
11	Number of Orders	20	1		Possible Unforeseen Demand in %	3%	Assumption
12	Total Variable Costs	550	28		Safety Stock	74	
13	Average Inventory	31	625		EOQ	62	
14	Total Holding Costs	558	8906		Average Inventory	105	
15	Total Inventory Costs	1108	8934		No of Orders per year	21	
16					Cost of Safety & EOQ	30	
17	Cost of goods to Supplier	75000	59375		Cost of EOQ without Safety Stock	9	
18	Total Costs	76108	68309				
19							
20	Saving/cost of supplier policy	7799					

Figure 11.9 Economic order quantity

cost as a percentage and the variable cost per order. Using the equation for EOQ described above the formula required in cell B8 is:

=ROUND(SQRT((2*B3*B5)/(B4*B6)),0)

The ROUND function has been incorporated in the above formula to ensure that the nearest whole number is returned as the EOQ.

EOQ with a supplier policy

One additional item of input is required for the calculation of the EOQ with a supplier policy and that is the minimum order requirement. For this example the unit price has been reduced from 60 to 47.50, but the supplier demands a minimum order of 1250 units. The formula required in cell C8 is therefore:

=ROUND(MAX(SQRT((2*C3*C5)/(C4*C6)),C7),0)

The MAX function in the above formula compares the result of the SQRT part of the calculation with the minimum order and returns the larger number. Therefore if the annual usage is very large it will be more economical to purchase more than 1250 units.

Cost of inventory

It is important to know the cost of inventory both with and without the supplier discount policy in order that a comparison can be made to ascertain whether it is worthwhile accepting the supplier discount. Figure 11.10 shows the formulae for this part of the plan.

	A	B	C
10	**Total Cost of Inventory**		
11	Number of Orders	=ROUND(B3/B8,0)	=ROUND(C3/C8,0)
12	Total Variable Costs	=B11*B5	=C11*C5
13	Average Inventory	=ROUND(B8/2,0)	=ROUND(C8/2,0)
14	Total Holding Costs	=B13*B4*B6	=C13*C4*C6
15	Total Inventory Costs	=B14+B12	=C14+C12
16			
17	Cost of goods to Supplier	=B3*B4	=C3*C4
18	Total Costs	=B17+B15	=C17+C15
19			
20	Saving/cost of supplier policy	=B18-C18	

Figure 11.10 Formulae for calculating the cost of inventory

As can be seen from Figure 11.10, although the cost of inventory is higher for the supplier policy scenario, the overall costs are still lower due to the lower selling price.

Lead times and safety stock

As it is likely that there will be a lead time between placing and receiving an order, this should be taken into consideration and a safety stock level be set which ensures that an order will be placed at the right time. The implications of this are calculated in the third part of this plan. Three further assumptions are made; the lead time in weeks, the possible delivery delay in weeks and the possible percentage unforeseen demand. The calculations here have been done for no supplier policy, but could equally well include the supplier policy. Figure 11.11 shows the formulae required for this part of the plan.

	E	F	G
1			
2	**With lead times and safety stock**		
3	Annual Usage in Units	=B3	
4	Weekly Usage	=F3/52	
5	Unit Price	=B4	
6	Variable Cost per Order	=B5	
7	Holding Cost as %	=B6	
8	Lead Time in Weeks	8	Assumption
9	Re-order Point	=F4*F8	
10	Possible Delivery Delay in Weeks	3	Assumption
11	Possible Unforeseen Demand in %	0.03	Assumption
12	Safety Stock	=(F4*F10)+(F4*F10*F11)	
13	**EOQ**	**=ROUND((SQRT((2*F3*F6)/(F5*F7)))+1,0)**	
14	Average Inventory	=F13/2+F12	
15	No of Orders per year	=ROUND((F3/F13)+1,0)	
16	Cost of Safety & EOQ	=(F13+F12/2)*F7	
17	Cost of EOQ without Safety Stock	=F13/2*F7	

Figure 11.11 Formulae for calculating lead times and safety stock

Sales campaign appraisal

The sales campaign appraisal model is a deterministic plan that evaluates the cost of conducting a promotional sales campaign over a number of weeks. The plan reports on the likely number of prospects that will attend sales presentations and how many will be converted to sales. The model is on the CD accompanying the book under the name CAMPAIGN.

The sales campaign plan has been designed for 10 weeks of analysis after the initial promotion and requires the following input:

◆ initial promotion cost
◆ duration of primary promotion in weeks
◆ cost of a sales presentation
◆ revenue per unit sold
◆ cost per unit
◆ conversion rate to sale at presentation as a percentage
◆ estimate of the percentage of enquiries converted to sales presentation
◆ estimate of the number of enquiries per week after promotion
◆ estimate of the number of prospects attending sales presentation who will eventually purchase.

Figure 11.12 shows the completed model with sample data.

	A	B	C	D	E	F	G	H	I	J	K	L
1	Sales Campaign Appraisal											
2												
3	Product				Widgets							
4	Initial promotion costs				155000							
5	Promotion duration in weeks				5							
6	Cost of sales presentation				775							
7	Conversion to sale at presentation %				40%							
8	Revenue per unit				3950							
9	Production cost per unit				1250							
10												
11	Weeks after promotion	No. of enquiries	Cum. enquiries	No. sales presentations	Cum. sales present's	Units sold	Cum. sales	Cost per presentation	Marketing cost per sale	Total cost	Total revenue	Profit on campaign
12	1	130	130	0	0	0	0	0				
13	2	190	320	47	47	18	18	4073	8611	213925	71100	-142825
14	3	250	570	67	114	26	44	1815	3523	261925	173800	-88125
15	4	440	1010	92	206	36	80	1099	1938	326300	316000	-10300
16	5	750	1760	142	348	56	136	762	1140	435050	537200	102150
17	6	555	2315	258	606	103	239	586	649	653700	944050	290350
18	7	300	2615	189	795	75	314	379	494	693975	1240300	546325
19	8	100	2715	93	888	37	351	256	442	665825	1386450	720625
20	9	25	2740	32	920	12	363	195	427	633550	1433850	800300
21	10	5	2745	8	928	3	366	174	423	618700	1445700	827000

CAMPAIGN.XLS

Figure 11.12 Sales campaign appraisal model

Developing the sales campaign plan

The first step in the plan is to enter all the headings so that there is a structure for the model. Some sample data should be entered in order that the logic for the formulae can be checked as it is being developed.

The number of enquiries received each week after the initial promotion is an estimate. In this example it is assumed that the effects of the promotion increase over a five-week period and then begin to drop off until there are only a few enquiries at the end of the ten weeks.

The estimated numbers of sales presentations are assumed to be linked with the numbers of enquiries. In this example it is estimated to be between 30 and 40% of the previous week's enquiries. The values in the model are derived by a random number generator used in conjunction with a one-period lag on the number of enquiries. The formula entered into cell D13, which is copied for the remaining weeks is:

=INT(RAND()*0.1)+0.3)*B12

The RAND function in the above formula generates a random number between 0 and 1. However, by manipulating the result as shown in the above formula the result will always be between 30 and 40% of the previous week's number of enquiries.

The problem with the RAND function is that it is re-evaluated every time the spreadsheet is recalculated and therefore different values will be returned. Therefore having produced a series of estimated values these cells should be converted to values only. This is achieved by copying the range with the Edit Copy command and then selecting Paste Special Values. This removes the underlying formula leaving only the results in the cells.

The units sold are calculated by multiplying the number of sales presentations by the conversion to sale percentage. The following formula is required in cell F13, which can be copied for the remaining weeks:

$$=\text{INT}(\text{D13}*\$\text{E}\$7)$$

The INT function has been incorporated into the formula to ensure that the result is rounded down to a whole number.

The cost per presentation is calculated by multiplying the cost per sales presentation by the number of presentations, adding that to the total cost of promotion and dividing by the cumulative sales presentation. The formula in cell H13, which is copied for the remaining weeks is:

$$=(\$\text{E}\$4+(\text{D13}*\$\text{E}\$6))/\text{E13}$$

The marketing cost per sale is the promotion cost divided by the cumulative sales, which means the following formula is required in cell I13:

$$=\$\text{E}\$4/\text{G13}$$

The total costs are calculated as the promotion costs plus the cost of the sales presentations that week plus the production costs for units sold. The formula required in cell J13 is therefore:

$$=\$\text{E}\$4+(\$\text{E}\$6*\text{D13})+(\text{G13}*\$\text{E}\$9)$$

The total revenue is the number of units sold multiplied by the revenue per unit and the profit on the campaign is therefore calculated as the total costs less the total revenue.

Summary

In this chapter a number of different business plans have been developed in order to demonstrate some of the applications for which a spreadsheet can be used. It is hoped that readers will find some of the models directly applicable but some of the techniques and functions shown can also be applied in a number of complimentary areas.

12

What-if Analysis

Good judgment is usually the result of experience. And experience is frequently the result of bad judgment.

— R.E. Neustadt and E.R. May, *Thinking in Time*, 1986.

Introduction

What-if analysis may be defined as the technique of asking specific questions about the result of a change or of a series of changes to assumptions in a model or a business plan.

What-if analysis has been performed manually for decades before the arrival of computers. In the spreadsheet environment, however, it is a direct product of the fact that once a model or plan has been entered into the computer, it may be recalculated again and again. It allows the user to change assumptions concerning input data or input relationships, and to recalculate a model to see the impact of these changes on critical output values.

Typical what-if questions might be to ask what effect will a 2% increase in direct labour costs have on profit and return on investment? What effect will a further 30 day delay in receiving cash from the debtors have on the overdraft and/or return on investment?

What-if questions may be considered one at a time, or several at a time. If it is necessary to investigate the effect of two simultaneous changes in the assumptions, then it is usually advantageous to also consider these changes in isolation, i.e. one at a time, so that their individual effects, as well as their joint effects, will be known. Irrespective of whether single or multiple changes to input are made, several factors or objectives will usually be monitored.

In addition to what-if analysis, there are two other related concepts which should also be considered. These are *goal seeking* or *backward iteration* and *sensitivity analysis*.

Goal seeking is a technique whereby a model calculates the value of an input variable that is required in order to achieve a stated output objective. For example, using goal seeking the system could calculate the level of sales required for a return on investment of 25%. Thus the goal-seeking procedure requires an input variable, which is usually considered the models' output, and the result is the value for a variable that is normally input to the model. Excel has a built-in command for this, which will be discussed later in this chapter.

Sensitivity analysis is a technique that ascertains the relative importance of specified input variables in a business scenario or plan. This is achieved by calculating the result of a number of relatively small changes in the specified input factors on the objective function, or output of the business model. These input and output changes are then compared to ascertain which variables have the greatest impact. The user of sensitivity analysis is concerned to establish whether a 5% increase in raw material costs, or a 2% increase in labour costs will have the worse impact on the profit of the business.

Sensitivity analysis and what-if analysis are quite different techniques, although the terms are often used interchangeably.

Three approaches to what-if analysis

With spreadsheet models there are several possible levels of what-if and associated analysis available, which can be described in terms of the following three categories:

1. manual what-if analysis on opening assumptions
2. data tables
3. backward iteration or goal seeking.

Each of these will be considered separately in this chapter.

Manual what-if analysis on opening assumptions

Manual what-if analysis on opening values is the simplest case and is performed by placing the cursor on the appropriate input cell and entering a new assumption. Because spreadsheets are developed using cell references, all cells which refer directly or indirectly to the cell being changed will be recalculated based on the revised input. Providing recalculation is set to automatic, the spreadsheet is immediately recalculated and the effect of the new assumption can be seen. This approach to the what-if technique is especially suitable when first-period data assumptions such as price, opening sales volumes, or growth factors and cost factors are to be changed.

Figure 12.1 shows the 12 month business plan that will be used throughout this chapter and Figure 12.2 shows the effect that reducing the opening sales volume has on the net profit. This plan can be found on the CD accompanying the book under the name **BUSPLAN.**

	A	B	C	D	E	F	G	H	I	J	K	L	M	N
1	12 month Business Plan													
2														
3		JAN	FEB	MAR	APR	MAY	JUN	JUL	AUG	SEP	OCT	NOV	DEC	TOTAL
4	Income													
5	Volume	9750	9849	9948	10049	10151	10254	10358	10462	10568	10675	10783	10893	123740
6	Unit Price	50	50	50	50	50	50	50	50	50	50	50	50	
7	Turnover	482625	487512	492448	497434	502470	507558	512697	517888	523131	528428	533778	539183	6125151
8														
9	Expenditure													
10	Raw Materials	190125	192050	193995	195959	197943	199947	201971	204016	206082	208169	210276	212405	2412938
11	Direct Labour	112750	112750	112750	112750	112750	112750	112750	112750	112750	112750	112750	112750	1353000
12	Energy Consumed	34125	34471	34820	35172	35528	35888	36251	36618	36989	37364	37742	38124	433091
13	Total Direct Costs	337000	339271	341564	343881	346221	348585	350973	353385	355821	358282	360768	363279	4199030
14	**Gross Profit**	145625	148241	150884	153553	156249	158973	161724	164503	167310	170146	173010	175903	1926121
15														
16	Other Costs													
17	Administration	14625	14773	14923	15074	15226	15381	15536	15694	15852	16013	16175	16339	185611
18	Commission	2413	2438	2462	2487	2512	2538	2563	2589	2616	2642	2669	2696	30626
19	Depreciation	19500	19697	19897	20098	20302	20507	20715	20925	21137	21351	21567	21785	247481
20	Interest	1200	1200	1200	1200	1200	1200	1200	1200	1200	1200	1200	1200	14400
21	Maintenance	3370	3393	3416	3439	3462	3486	3510	3534	3558	3583	3608	3633	41990
22	Salaries	75000	75000	75000	75000	75000	75000	75000	75000	75000	75000	75000	75000	900000
23	Travel	4550	4550	4550	4550	4550	4550	4550	4550	4550	4550	4550	4550	54600
24	Total Other Costs	120658	121051	121447	121848	122253	122662	123074	123492	123913	124339	124768	125203	1474708
25														
26	**Net Profit B. Tax**	24967	27190	29436	31705	33996	36311	38650	41011	43397	45807	48242	50701	451414
27														
28	Growth rates and cost factors													
29	Volume	1.01%												
30	Price	0.00%												
31	Raw Material Costs	19.50												
32	Energy cost per unit	3.50												
33	Admin cost per unit	1.50												
34	Commission %	0.50%												
35	Depreciation per unit	2												
36	Maintenance as % of costs	1.00%												

Figure 12.1 Business plan before performing what-if analysis

	A	B	C	D	E	F	G	H	I	J	K	L	M	N
1	12 month Business Plan													
2														
3		JAN	FEB	MAR	APR	MAY	JUN	JUL	AUG	SEP	OCT	NOV	DEC	TOTAL
4	Income													
5	Volume	8000	8081	8163	8245	8329	8413	8498	8585	8671	8759	8848	8938	101531
6	Unit Price	50	50	50	50	50	50	50	50	50	50	50	50	
7	Turnover	396000	400010	404060	408151	412283	416458	420674	424934	429236	433582	437972	442407	5025765
8														
9	Expenditure													
10	Raw Materials	156000	157580	159175	160787	162415	164059	165720	167398	169093	170805	172534	174281	1979847
11	Direct Labour	112750	112750	112750	112750	112750	112750	112750	112750	112750	112750	112750	112750	1353000
12	Energy Consumed	28000	28284	28570	28859	29151	29446	29745	30046	30350	30657	30968	31281	355357
13	Total Direct Costs	296750	298613	300495	302396	304316	306256	308215	310194	312193	314212	316252	318313	3688204
14	**Gross Profit**	99250	101397	103565	105755	107967	110202	112459	114740	117043	119370	121720	124094	1337561
15														
16	Other Costs													
17	Administration	12000	12122	12244	12368	12493	12620	12748	12877	13007	13139	13272	13406	152296
18	Commission	1980	2000	2020	2041	2061	2082	2103	2125	2146	2168	2190	2212	25129
19	Depreciation	16000	16162	16326	16491	16658	16827	16997	17169	17343	17518	17696	17875	203061
20	Interest	1200	1200	1200	1200	1200	1200	1200	1200	1200	1200	1200	1200	14400
21	Maintenance	2968	2986	3005	3024	3043	3063	3082	3102	3122	3142	3163	3183	36882
22	Salaries	75000	75000	75000	75000	75000	75000	75000	75000	75000	75000	75000	75000	900000
23	Travel	4550	4550	4550	4550	4550	4550	4550	4550	4550	4550	4550	4550	54600
24	Total Other Costs	113698	114020	114345	114674	115006	115341	115680	116022	116368	116717	117070	117426	1386368
25														
26	**Net Profit B. Tax**	-14448	-12623	-10780	-8919	-7039	-5139	-3221	-1283	675	2652	4650	6667	-48807
27														
28	Growth rates and cost factors													
29	Volume	1.01%												
30	Price	0.00%												
31	Raw Material Costs	19.50												
32	Energy cost per unit	3.50												
33	Admin cost per unit	1.50												
34	Commission %	0.50%												
35	Depreciation per unit	2												
36	Maintenance as % of costs	1.00%												

Figure 12.2 Business plan after reducing opening volume

BUSPLAN.XLS

Providing any growth or cost factors have been separated from the model, any input assumption can be changed using this technique. Furthermore if a data input form has been created as was shown in Chapter 9, it is easier to see the input data that can be changed.

Of course in some situations it may be necessary to make multiple changes to the data to derive a particular result. In this case it can be difficult to know which change is having the greatest impact on the result. In addition care needs to be taken not to accidentally overwrite the file if it is still required in the pre-what-if version.

Occasionally it might be necessary to see the effect of changing the actual logic of a plan. Extreme care must be taken in this case because changing the logic of plans that have been tried and tested can have knock-on effects that might not be obvious to the individual making the changes.

Data tables

Excel provides a powerful what-if facility referred to as *data tables*. Data tables allow a range of what-if questions to be calculated at one time, by setting up a table in which a range of possible input values are specified together with a reference to required output. For example, a data table can be established to report the effect of changing the sales volume growth rate on the gross profit, net profit, return on investment and cash in bank for all integer growth rates of sales volume between 0.5 and 10%. A key advantage to managing what-if questions with data tables is that the table sits alongside the original plan, which is not altered in any way.

There are two main types of data table, which are referred to as the one-way table and the two-way table. A one-way table allows a single input factor to be analysed against as many output variables as the user requires. The input factor is a cell in the plan that is to change and the output variables are those cells on which you want to see the effect of the change. For example, in the business plan used as the example in this chapter, the input factor might be the opening volume and the output variables might be the gross profit and net profit figures for July and December.

In the case of a two-way table, two input factors and a single output variable can be specified. In the business plan for example, the input factors might be the opening sales volume and the opening price and the output variable might be the year-end net profit.

Creating a one-way data table

In the case of a one-way data table, a range of input values must first be entered into a suitable area of the spreadsheet, and references to the formulae on which the analysis is to be performed must be made.

Figure 12.3 shows the outline of a table to analyse varying volume rates against the gross profit and net profit before tax for December in the business plan.

N.B. Remember to re-load the original BUSPLAN.XLS before commencing this exercise.

	A	B	C	D
40				
41		G. Profit	N. Profit	
42		175903	50701	
43	8000			
44	8250			
45	8500			
46	8750			
47	9000			
48	9250			
49	9500			
50	9750			
51	10000			
52	10250			
53	10500			
54				

BUSPLAN.XLS

Figure 12.3 Outline of a one-way data table

The values in the range A43 through A53 can be entered either by typing in the values, using a Fill technique or they maybe the result of a formula. In this example the values are in ascending order at regular intervals, but this is not necessary for the command to work. Cells B42 and C42 contain references to cells M14 and M26 in the business plan, which are the gross profit and net profit figures for December.

The next step is to highlight the table range, which in this case is A42 through C53. The DATA TABLE command is then selected which will bring up the dialogue box shown in Figure 12.4.

	A	B	C	D	E	F	G	H
1	**Business Plan**							
2								
3		JAN	FEB	MAR	APR	MAY	JUN	JUL
4	*Income*							
5	Volume	9750	9849	9948	10049	10151	10254	10358
6	Unit Price	50	50	50	50	50	50	50
7	**Turnover**	482625					58	512697
8	*Expenditure*		Row Input Cell:			OK		
9	Raw Materials	190125					47	201971
10	Direct Labour	112750	Column Input Cell:	B5		Cancel	50	112750
11	Energy Consumed	34125					38	36251
12	Total Direct Costs	337000					35	350973
13	**Gross Profit**	145625					73	161724
14	*Other Costs*							

Figure 12.4 Excel data table dialogue box

This example is a one-way table and the input data is referenced in a column. Therefore it is necessary to make a reference to the cell in the main model into which the input values are to be entered. In this case, a reference to the opening volume in cell B5 is required.

On clicking OK the table is calculated and will be displayed as shown in Figure 12.5.

	A	B	C	D
37				
38	Data Table to see the effect of changing sales volume			
39	on gross and net profit for December			
40				
41			**G. Profit**	**N. Profit**
42			175903	50701
43		8000	124094	6667
44		8250	131495	12958
45		8500	138897	19248
46		8750	146298	25539
47		9000	153699	31829
48		9250	161101	38120
49		9500	168502	44410
50		9750	175903	50701
51		10000	183305	56991
52		10250	190706	63282
53		10500	198108	69572

Figure 12.5 Results of a one-way data table

The results produced by the table is the equivalent of having entered 8000 into cell B5 and then recording the gross profit and net profit figures for December, then 8250 is entered into cell B5 and the gross profit and net profit figures for December is again recorded. This reiterative process would continue until all the required values for sales volume had been entered and the profit results recorded. The DATA TABLE command performs this reiteration extremely quickly.

As has been mentioned previously, it is important to always have a way of cross-checking the results of any analysis in order to validate the figures. The table in Figure 12.5 can be checked by looking at row 41 which gives the results when the opening volume is 9750 – as it is in the main plan – and these values should correspond to the results in cells B33 and C33. It can be seen from Figure 12.5 that the results do correspond.

Creating a two-way data table

A two-way data table requires input data for two variables. For example, to analyse a combined variation of opening sales volume figures and unit prices on the net profit before tax in December in the business plan, the table specifications in Figure 12.6 are required. In this case only one ouput variable is allowed – which is a reference to cell M26 (December net Profit) in cell B60.

	A	B	C	D	E	F	G	H	I
55									
56	Data Table to see the effect of changing sales volume								
57	and unit price on the net profit for December								
58									
59					Unit Price				
60		50701	35	40	45	50	55	60	
61		8000							
62		8250							
63		8500							
64	V	8750							
65	o	9000							
66	i	9250							
67	u	9500							
68	m	9750							
69	e	10000							
70		10250							
71		10500							
72									

Figure 12.6 Input data for a two-way data table

The table area is selected in the same way as for the one-way table, but when the dialogue box is accessed it is necessary this time to specify the column input cell as the sales volume in cell B5, and the row input cell as the unit price in cell B6. The results of this table are shown in Figure 12.7.

	A	B	C	D	E	F	G	H	I
55									
56	Data Table to see the effect of changing sales volume								
57	and unit price on the net profit for December								
58									
59					Unit Price				
60			50701	35	40	45	50	55	60
61			8000	-122278	-77814	-33350	11114	55578	100042
62			8250	-120017	-74164	-28310	17543	63397	109250
63			8500	-117757	-70513	-23270	23973	71216	118459
64		V	8750	-115496	-66863	-18230	30402	79035	127667
65		o	9000	-113235	-63213	-13191	36832	86854	136876
66		l	9250	-110974	-59562	-8151	43261	94673	146084
67		u	9500	-108713	-55912	-3111	49690	102491	155293
68		m	9750	-106452	-52261	1929	56120	110310	164501
69		e	10000	-104191	-48611	6969	62549	118129	173709
70			10250	-101930	-44961	12009	68979	125948	182918
71			10500	-99669	-41310	17049	75408	133767	192126
72									

Figure 12.7 Completed two-way data table

The results of this table are interesting, as it is clear that if the unit price is reduced to £45, a minimum of 9500 units must be produced to be in profit by the end of the year. But, if the price can be held at 50, the opening sales volume can be as little at 8000 and still leave a net profit at the end of the year.

In validating the accuracy of this table by taking a sales volume figure of 9750 and a price of 50, which is apparently the data in the main model, the resulting net profit in the table should be the same as the net profit in the model (which is shown in cell A55 of the table). Looking at the table, this is not the case as the net profit is showing 56,120 as opposed to the 50,701 that would be expected. Closer examination of the main plan will show that the unit price is actually 49.5, but the row has been formatted to a whole number and it therefore displaying 50. If the opening price in the model is changed to 50, the net profit for December in the model will be 56,120 as it is in the table.

Unusually the Data Table command places a formula using the TABLE function into each of the cells in the table range. Therefore if any changes are made to data in the main plan, or to the input or output ranges, the table will automatically be recalculated to reflect the changes. This also means that there can be multiple data tables on a spreadsheet and all can be kept up to date simultaneously. In fact sometimes when working with large tables, or many tables, it is not always desirable to have the tables recalculate every time an adjustment is made to the main plan and therefore by selecting TOOLS OPTIONS CALCULATIONS and then selecting Automatic except Tables means that it will be necessary to press F9 to recalculate the data tables.

One possible disadvantage of using data tables in Excel is the fact that they need to be located on the same worksheet as the input data, which effectively means that it is not possible to have a separate worksheet on which all the data tables for an application are placed.

Backward iteration or goal seeking

Having developed a business plan for the purposes of profit planning, the results calculated are not always entirely satisfactory to the decision makers. A typical example might be when the profit plan shows a projected 10% return on investment (ROI), but the management require a 15% ROI. In these circumstances what-if analysis can be performed on the basic assumptions in the model, in order to determine what volume of sales, for example, would be required to achieve the desired ROI for the business.

This procedure can, however, be a lengthy one if a large number of changes to the assumptions have to be made before the model produces the required results. An alternative method of finding appropriate input values for a required result or outcome are to use the Goalseek and Solver tools provided by Excel.

Using the goal seeking feature

In the original business plan the net profit in December is £50,701. The Goal Seek command can be used, for example, to consider what opening sales volume would be required in order for the December net profit to be £60,000 (taking all the other assumptions made in the plan into consideration).

Goal Seek is accessed by selecting TOOLS GOAL SEEK and the dialogue box shown in Figure 12.8 is displayed and has to be filled out with the appropriate information.

	B	C	D	E	F	G	H	I	J
4									
5	9750	9849	9948	10049	10151	10254	10358	10462	10568
6	50	50	50	50	50	50	50	50	50
7	482625	487512	492448	497434	502470	507558	512697	517888	523131
8									
9									
10	190125	192050	19399						206082
11	112750	112750	11275						112750
12	34125	34471	3482						36989
13	337000	339271	34156						355821
14	145625	148241	15088						167310
15									
16									
17	14625	14773	14923	15074	15226	15381	15536	15694	15852

Goal Seek dialog box: Set cell $M$26 — To value 60000 — By changing cell B5 — [OK] [Cancel]

Figure 12.8 Excel Goal Seek dialogue box

On clicking OK the spreadsheet is recalculated and the opening volume required in order to attain a year-end net profit of £60,000 is displayed in cell B5. In this case the answer is 10,120.

Goalseek is a quick to apply and useful tool, but is limited in functionality because it can only be applied to a single variable and the target value must be set as an actual value – no formulae reference or conditions are possible.

Use Solver for optimising

If a more complex analysis is required, the SOLVER command may be useful. With Solver a number of different cells in different parts of the spreadsheet can be changed and constraints can be specified to ensure certain parameters are met, such as units produced in a production model cannot exceed a given number or advertising expenditure cannot be a negative value. The output cell can be a specified value or it can be the maximum possible solution or the minimum possible solution, so that, for example, the maximum profit for varying units of production can be found or the minimum profit within the same constraints could be returned.

Solver requires the model to be set up with the required data and constraints before the analysis can be performed. Figure 12.9

shows a salesman's productivity model that will be used in this example. This file can be found on the CD accompanying this book under the name **SALESMAN.** The aim is to find the maximum profit that can be made by the sales team. Note that the constraints in Figure 12.9 are at this stage only text entries for information purposes.

	A	B	C	D
1	SALESMAN'S PRODUCTIVITY MODEL			
2				
3		NO. OF	PROFIT	TOTAL
4	SALESMAN	SALES	PER SALE	PROFIT
5	Higgins	40	30	1200
6	Dolittle	40	45	1800
7	Spock	40	25	1000
8	Jekyll	30	36	1080
9	TOTAL	150		5080
10				
11				
12	CONSTRAINTS			
13	Higgins	Minimum quota is 20 sales		
14	Dolittle	Minimum quota is 10 sales		
15	Spock	Minimum quota is 30 sales		
16	Jekyll	Minimum quota is 25 sales		
17	Total	Total number of sales must be 150		

Figure 12.9 Salesman's productivity model before optimising

Each sales person has a minimum quota that he or she is required to attain and the firm is dependent on a total sales figure of 150 units. Each sales person is responsible for a different product and the profit per sale, which is different for each product, has been entered into the model in column C. The adjustable cells are B5 through B8 which represent the number of sales per person.

Some values must be entered into these cells before using Solver, but they will be replaced during the analysis.

Having set up the spreadsheet, TOOLS SOLVER is selected and the Solver Parameters dialogue box is displayed as shown in Figure 12.10.

The *target* cell is the total sales in cell D9 and the intention is to *maximise* this value by *changing* cells B5 through B8. These changes are *subject to the constraints* that have been specified on the spreadsheet in Figure 12.11.

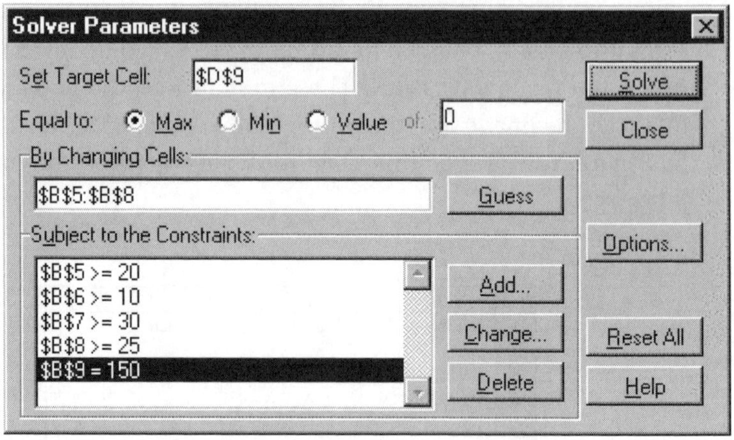

Figure 12.10 Excel Solver dialogue box

	A	B	C	D
1	SALESMAN'S PRODUCTIVITY MODEL			
2				
3		NO. OF	PROFIT	TOTAL
4	SALESMAN	SALES	PER SALE	PROFIT
5	Higgins	20	30	600
6	Dolittle	75	45	3375
7	Spock	30	25	750
8	Jekyll	25	36	900
9	TOTAL	150		5625
10				
11				
12	CONSTRAINTS			
13	Higgins	Minimum quota is 20 sales		
14	Dolittle	Minimum quota is 10 sales		
15	Spock	Minimum quota is 30 sales		
16	Jekyll	Minimum quota is 25 sales		
17	Total	Total number of sales must be 150		

Figure 12.11 Spreadsheet after using Solver

Figure 12.11 shows the spreadsheet after *Solve* is selected from the dialogue box.

It is sometimes possible to specify a problem that has no solution, which means that there is no set of adjustable cell values that will satisfy all of the constraints made. For example, if an additional constraint of total profit to be greater than 10,000 is added to the above example, Solver attempts to find a solution and then reports that no feasible answer could be found.

The example used here to illustrate Solver is a simple one and serves merely as an introduction to a feature that can perform very sophisticated analysis. Possible applications include solving simultaneous linear and non-linear equations, optimising investment yield, production level planning, staff scheduling models, etc.

Summary

The ability to perform what-if analysis on a business plan provides the necessary flexibility that enables financial managers and accountants to become power users of Excel. The speed of recalculation and the ease of change make this perhaps the single most important reason for the success of spreadsheet technology. It is important to remember, however, that the success of any kind of what-if or sensitivity analysis is entirely dependent on the correct development of the basic plan and the ability to interpret what the results might mean.

The goal seeking and solver features allow for powerful optimising techniques to be applied to a range of business plans.

Risk Analysis

There is an intrinsic impermanence in industry and indeed the management task is to recreate the company in a new form every year.

— Sir John Harvey-Jones, *Making it Happen – Reflections on Leadership*, 1988.

Introduction

Most business plans are deterministic, which means that they rely on the use of single point estimates for input data and assumptions. Under conditions of uncertainty, which is the most common environment in which business plans are developed, it can be difficult to produce accurate estimates using a single point approach and in such situations it would be preferable to specify input data as ranges.

For example, to say that the sales volume for the next period will be between 8500 and 12,500 will offer a greater probability of being right than a single point estimate of, say, 10,000. Similarly, to specify the average sales price as being between 45 and 52 will often have a greater chance of producing useful results than having to depend on a single projection of 50.

The structure of a deterministic plan, by its very nature, cannot cope with input data specified as ranges. However, it is possible to develop a model which enhances a deterministic, single-point estimate plan to allow data in the form of ranges to be incorporated, and which in effect converts the plan from a deterministic to a *probabilistic, stochastic* or *risk analysis* model. Risk analysis is also sometimes called probabilistic modelling, stochastic modelling or Monte Carlo modelling.

The principle of this type of modelling is to produce a probability distribution of the required result. This is achieved by randomly selecting values between the specified ranges and collecting the result after each calculation. This recalculation of the plan is repeated many times (hundreds or thousands) and a frequency distribution is then calculated on the output. The results of probabilistic plans are usually best accessed in the form of a chart and by examining the shape of the curve and the extent of the spread of the output.

For example, to see the effect of a range of input data for the investment amount in the CIA model on the NPV at a fixed interest rate, it would be necessary to recalculate the model using different

investment amounts and to collect the NPV result for each calculation. After a considerable number of recalculations, preferably
thousands, a frequency distribution of the results is created and a
graph is drawn. This graph will, in general, be a bell-shaped curve
and the precise shape of the curve will reflect the degree of risk
that is present in the investment based on the input data ranges.

Preparing a plan for risk analysis

It is usual to begin risk analysis from a fully tested deterministic plan
or model. This is because it is difficult to develop a plan and be able
to test the results of the underlying logic when ranges of data are used.

However, by carefully designing the original plan it is not difficult
to adapt it for risk analysis and the example in this chapter uses the
CIA plan developed in Chapter 11.

The completed risk analysis model will use four separate worksheets. The first sheet, called *CIA Model*, is the original CIA plan.
The amended data from the original plan is on a sheet called *Risk
Model*, the input form worksheet is called *Input*, the risk analysis
results worksheet is called *Results* and the chart is on a worksheet
called *Risk Chart*. The file can be found on the CD accompanying
this book under the name RISK.

Changing the original plan

Two changes are required to the basic plan. These are for the input
form to accommodate ranges of data and for the logic of the plan to
incorporate a random number generator using the range data.

RISK.XLS

The selection of the data for insertion in the plan is based on either a
probability distribution or, in the case of the risk analysis described
in this book, a random number generator. The specification of probability distributions for risk analysis is beyond the scope of this
book, and thus it is assumed that the data will be specified as simple
maximum and minimum values and that all possible obtainable
results are of equal probability. This is referred to in statistical jargon
as *rectangular distributions*.

Figure 13.1 shows the data input form for risk analysis on the CIA
model. For this example the variable data is the investment amount,

	A	B	C	D	E	F	G	H	I	J	K	L	M
1	Input form for Risk Analysis												
2				Minimum	Maximum								
3	IT Investment - Cash Out			350000	400000								
4													
5	Net IT Benefits	Year 1		60000	70000								
6		Year 2		95000	105000								
7		Year 3		120000	130000								
8		Year 4		180000	200000								
9		Year 5		200000	250000								
10													
11	Fixed Cost of Capital			20.00%	30.00%								
12													
13	Inflation adjusted cost of capital			Y1 Min	Y1 Max	Y2 Min	Y2 Max	Y3 Min	Y3 Max	Y4 Min	Y4 Max	Y5 Min	Y5 Max
14				20%	25%	30%	35%	35%	40%	40%	45%	45%	50%
15													
16													
17	Select variable to report				NPV (FDR)	-67077							
18	with an X in the appropriate box			X	IRR	19.85%							
19					NPV (VDR)	-86502							
20													
21				N.B. You must mark ONLY ONE box with an upper case X									
22													
23													

CIA Model / Risk Model \ Input / Results / Riskchart / Sheet5 / Sheet6 /

Ready   Sum=0

Figure 13.1 Input form for risk analysis

the cash-in flows, the fixed and the inflation adjusted discount rates. When entering data for the risk analysis it may not be appropriate to use all these variables and in this case the same value can be entered for the minimum and the maximum value. In this example, an option for performing risk analysis on three variables has been given. These are NPV at a fixed interest rate, IRR and NPV at a variable discount rate.

Cells and ranges in the output selection part of the input form need to be named for future reference in the *Results* sheet. Therefore using the Insert Name Define command names representing the three variables that the risk analysis can be performed on are assigned as follows:

E17   NPVF

E18   IRR

E19   NPVV

References to the formulae for these variables in the main model on the *Risk Model* sheet should be entered into cells F17, F18 and F19 as follows:

F17   ='RISK MODEL'!C19

F18   ='RISK MODEL'!C21

F19   ='RISK MODEL'!C24

At this point, cells F17, F18 and F19 will be displaying the current values for the net present value, the IRR and the net present value at a variable discount rate. As it is not necessary for the user to see the value in these cells, selecting them and changing the font colour to white can hide them.

The range D17 through F19 is named '*looktab*' and will be referenced as a lookup table in the *Results* sheet.

Incorporating the RAND function

In order to select values at random from within the specified ranges the referencing cells in the main model use the RAND function in the following way:

INT(RAND * (MAXIMUM − MINIMUM) + MINIMUM)

The RAND function generates a value between 0 and 1, never actually being 0 or 1. Looking at Figure 13.1 the range of values for the investment has been specified as between 350,000 and 400,000 and so if RAND returned a value of 0.56125, the above formula would calculate as:

INTEGER OF (0.56125 * (400,000 − 350,000) + 350,000)

which will give an answer of 378,062. In fact the result will always be a value between the specified ranges.

Figure 13.2 shows some of the formulae in the main model incorporating the random number generator.

	A	B	C
1	Capital Investment Appraisal System		
2			
3		Cash-Out	Cash-In
4	IT Investment - Cash Out	=INT(RAND()*(Input!E3-Input!D3)+Input!D3)	
5	Net IT Benefits Year 1		=INT(RAND()*(Input!E5-Input!D5)+Input!D5)
6	Year 2		=INT(RAND()*(Input!E6-Input!D6)+Input!D6)
7	Year 3		=INT(RAND()*(Input!E7-Input!D7)+Input!D7)
8	Year 4		=INT(RAND()*(Input!E8-Input!D8)+Input!D8)
9	Year 5		=INT(RAND()*(Input!E9-Input!D9)+Input!D9)
10			
11	Fixed Cost of Capital or Interest Rate		=(RAND()*(Input!E11-Input!D11)+Input!D11)
12			
13			Y1
14	Forecast inflation rates		=RAND()*(Input!E14-Input!D14)+Input!D14
15			
16	Investment Reports on IT System		
17	Payback in years & months		=B37
18	Rate of return(%)		=AVERAGE(C5:C9)/ABS(B4)
19	N P V Fixed Discount Rate (FDR)		=NPV(C11,C5:C9)-B4
20	Profitability Index FDR (PI)		=NPV(C11,C5:C9)/B4
21	Internal Rate of Return (IRR)		=IRR(E4:E9,0.3)
22			

Figure 13.2 Incorporating a random number generator

The system generates a different random number every time the spreadsheet is recalculated and thus by pressing F9 a different set of values will be returned in the main model and in turn the investment reports will be recalculated using different data each time.

The results worksheet

The results of recalculating the model are collected on the *results* worksheet together with some summary statistics and a frequency distribution table. Figure 13.3 shows a section of the results spreadsheet after performing the analysis on the IRR.

	A	B	C	D	E	F	G	H
1	Risk analysis results - Press F9 to recalculate							
2								
3		IRR		Summary statistics for	IRR		Frequency Table	
4		0.17						IRR
5	1	0.21		Mean	0.20		0.164	1
6	2	0.21		Standard Deviation	0.02		0.172	30
7	3	0.22		Range	0.08		0.180	124
8	4	0.21		Minimum	0.16		0.188	257
9	5	0.22		Maximum	0.24		0.196	290
10	6	0.21		Count	2000.00		0.204	289
11	7	0.23					0.212	321
12	8	0.22					0.219	315
13	9	0.18					0.227	233
14	10	0.23					0.235	113
15	11	0.20					0.243	27
16	12	0.22						

Figure 13.3 Results worksheet

In order that the risk analysis will be performed on the variable marked with an X on the Input worksheet, formulae are required in cells B3 and B4. A VLOOKUP function is used in both cases. Cell B3 is a reference to the variable label and the following formula is required:

=IF(ISERR(VLOOKUP("X",LOOKTAB,2)),"MAKE A SELECTION",
    VLOOKUP("X",LOOKTAB,2))

The VLOOKUP in this formula looks for X in the first column of the table range *looktab* and returns the contents of the cell one column to the right. If something other than X is entered, the VLOOKUP function will return an error. For this reason the formula begins with ISERR which means that if the result of the VLOOKUP is an error, the text "Make a selection" will be returned, otherwise the result of the VLOOKUP function will be returned, which in the case of Figure 13.3 is IRR.

A similar formula is required in cell B4 to pick up the cell reference to the variable data which in the case of Figure 13.3 is 0.18:

=VLOOKUP("X",LOOKTAB,3)

The labels in cells E3 and H4 are references to cell B3.

Collecting the results

The results of the risk analysis will be collected using a data table. The more reiterations of the model the better the results, and so for this example the plan has been set up to perform 2000 recalculations, thus collecting 2000 different results. Numbers 1 through 2000 are entered into cells A5 through A2004. To calculate the table the range A4 through B2004 is highlighted and the Table command selected by Data Table. This is a one-way table requiring column input and the reference can be to any blank cell, such as A3. When OK is clicked the table is calculated by placing the number 1 in cell A3, recalculating the model and placing the resulting IRR in cell B5. The number 2 is then entered in cell A3, the model is recalculated, which due to the RAND function causes all input and output to change and a different IRR is placed in cell B6. The computer continues this process 2000 times at which point there are 2000 IRR results in the range B5 through B2004.

Note that it is important at this point to set recalculation to Automatic except Tables from the Tools Calculation box otherwise the table will be recalculated every time something is entered into the spreadsheet.

Summary statistics

Some useful statistics about the results have been entered into the range D5 through E10. To make the referencing of the data easier the range B5 through B2004 is named 'output'. A range is named by selecting the required range and then clicking on the name box located to the left of the edit line at the top of the screen and typing in the name. The following formulae have been entered into column E:

E5	=AVERAGE(OUTPUT)
E6	=STDEV(OUTPUT)
E7	=E9–E8
E8	=MIN(OUTPUT)
E9	=MAX(OUTPUT)
E10	=COUNT(OUTPUT)

The results of the risk analysis are most clearly viewed on a chart, but 2000 data points are too many to plot onto a graph. Therefore a frequency distribution of the data is created and a graph is drawn using this data.

For this example, 11 data points have been chosen, beginning with the minimum value returned as a result and then 10 further points at equal intervals finishing with the maximum value returned as a result. This is achieved with the following formulae in cells G5 and G6:

G5	E8
G6	G5+($E$7*0.1)

The formula in cell G6 is then copied to cell G15.

Frequency distribution

The FREQUENCY function is used to return the number of times the results fall between the specified ranges. The form of the FREQUENCY command in cell H5 is:

$={FREQUENCY(B5:B2004,G5:G15)}$

The {} brackets mean this is an *array* function and as such has to be entered in a special way. First, using the mouse select the range in which the formulae are required – H5 through H15. Type in the formula *without* the {} brackets. Then enter the formula by holding the CTRL key and pressing SHIFT ENTER. The full range will be calculated in one operation.

Displaying the results on a chart

The results can be displayed graphically by selecting the range G4 through H15 and using the Chart button to automatically create a chart such as the one shown in Figure 13.4.

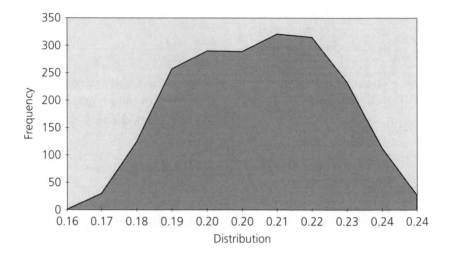

Figure 13.4 Graphical results of risk analysis on IRR

This graph illustrates quite a low level of risk because the most likely outcome is a return of 21.20% with a standard deviation of 1.6%. Furthermore, even if all the most unfavourable estimates occur, i.e. maximum investment costs, lowest cash-in flows and highest cost of capital, this investment will still be expected to produce an IRR of 16.4%. On the other hand, if the investment is kept low and the highest cash-in flows are achieved with a low cost of capital, this investment could produce a return of 24.3%.

N.B. Due to the use of the RAND function the results of this exercise will never be exactly the same as those displayed here.

Using the risk analysis model

Having set the risk analysis model up as shown in this chapter it can be used with different ranges of input data, in this example to analyse varying investment amounts with different cash flow and discount rate scenarios. By putting an X in the appropriate box in the input sheet the analysis can be performed on the NPV at a fixed discount rate, the IRR or the NPV at a variable discount rate. If it is only appropriate to specify ranges for some of the input variables the same value can be entered for the minimum and maximum in the input sheet.

To recalculate the model after new input data has been entered or a different output variable has been selected, F9 is pressed which recalculates the data table and the remaining formulae cells are also re-evaluated.

Summary

The risk of any investment is the potential for input and/or output variables to fluctuate from their original estimates. Risk analysis accommodates this uncertainty by allowing ranges, as opposed to single point estimates, to be used. It is generally easier to confidently state that an investment will be between 300,000 and 400,000 than to say it will be 380,000.

The methodology applied to this example can be used with most well designed deterministic plans.

Part 3

Budgeting

You can fool all the people all the time if the advertising is right and the budget is big enough.

— Joseph E. Levine, quoted in *Halliwell's Filmgoer's Companion*, 1984.

Introduction

A budget is a detailed estimate of future transactions. It can be expressed in terms of physical quantities, money or both. The essence of a budget is that it is a target set for management to keep within, achieve or surpass. Thus, a budget is always associated with a specific departmental responsibility point or centre within the organisation. This might be a division that has a sales budget, a factory with a capital budget or an individual with an expense budget.

Scope of budgeting

Budgetary control is not limited to commercial and industrial firms attempting to produce a profit. The procedures involved are equally applicable to *not-for-profit* organisations such as government departments, universities and charities.

All aspects of the business or organisation can be budgeted. There might be *income and expenditure* budgets, *cash* budgets, *capital* budgets, *research and development* budgets to mention only a few examples. Budgets can be classified as *master* budgets, *departmental* budgets or *functional* budgets. Whatever level or degree of detail, a budget is useless if it does not focus on a point of responsibility.

Budgeting is a management function that incorporates:

◆ setting objectives
◆ establishing detailed financial estimates
◆ delegating specific responsibility
◆ monitoring performance
◆ reacting to expectations.

Benefits of budgeting

The benefits of budgetary control can usefully be classified in the following way:

◆ A budget forces management to express in figures its future intentions.
◆ It provides a yardstick by which individuals or groups can be measured and rewarded.
◆ It allows some responsibility and authority to be decentralised without loss of information required by management for control purposes.
◆ Budgeting provides a mechanism to control in detail the revenue, costs, cash and capital expenditure of the firm.
◆ It facilitates an atmosphere of cost consciousness.
◆ It helps ensure that ROI is optimised.

Different approaches to budgeting

There are various approaches to the preparation of a budgeting system, but two popular methods are the *traditional approach* and the *zero-based budgeting approach.*

With the traditional approach some organisations re-compile last year's or the previous period's figures, adjusted for expected growth or for inflation. This approach to formulating a budget relies on the notion that all the business variables will remain more or less the same in relation to one another from one period to the next. For this type of budget, after preparing an initial set of figures, a minimal amount of maintenance is required.

On the other hand, some organisations adopt the view that the most important aspect of budgetary control lies in the fact that the creation of budgets should impose on the firm a strict regime of thinking through what the organisation is doing and where it is going. This approach has been popularised under the title of zero-based budgeting (ZBB) and assumes that it is necessary to start the budgeting process from scratch each time. The main advantage of this approach is that is ensures a rethink of the basic business assumptions on which the organisation relies. With a ZBB system, each functional section in the business will plan in detail all revenue, expenditure and capital items and these items will be ranked in order of importance to the firm.

An outcome from a ZBB system that is not the case with the traditional approach is that management are forced to prove the need for each item of expenditure in the budget. It is not good enough to say that the promotion account had a particular amount in it last year and that this figure should be increased by 10% for inflation. Clearly, it is more expensive to operate a ZBB system than a traditional system, and therefore a cost-benefit study is appropriate before embarking on a ZBB.

The term 'ZBB' is generally associated with the budgeting of indirect costs. It is therefore used extensively in central service departments, marketing and distribution, and research and development. ZBB is not considered to be directly relevant to the manufacturing process, as detailed expenditure in this area is usually automatically accounted for on a variable or direct basis.

Budget preparation

The procedure and operation of any budgetary control system is clearly specific to each individual organisation and is a function of management style and corporate culture. However, there are general guidelines that are useful to bear in mind:

◆ Establishing the objectives – This usually involves a lengthy process of analysing the organisations' strengths and weaknesses and matching these to the opportunities in the environment in which the organisation functions. This is sometimes referred to as *strategic planning*. This is a senior management activity which is an ongoing process coming to a focal point at budget time. A top-down approach is normally dominant here.

◆ Forecasting the key business variables – Before any figures can be derived an activity forecast must be established. In many organisations this means that a sales forecast must be produced which can be a lengthy and difficult process. It is important to ensure that a broad spectrum of people are involved and committed to the sales forecast. Therefore both top-down and bottom-up approaches are appropriate here.

- ◆ Physical estimates are calculated – The number of people, the scale of equipment and the volumes of raw materials required must be established. This is usually a bottom-up procedure.
- ◆ Detailed costings of each responsibility centre are made – This requires the involvement of a wide variety of staff and can lead to a considerable amount of negotiation. Thus, both top-down and bottom-up approaches are required.

These activities are best conducted in a cyclical fashion with feedback being sent up and down the organisation at various times, representing how different groups feel about the suggestions being made. Thus, the amount of time required to produce a budget can be substantial.

Spreadsheets for budgets

A spreadsheet can be used to support both the traditional approach to budgeting as well as the zero-based approach.

With the traditional approach, having initially designed and developed a plan with care, continuous use of the system is largely a case of changing the input data. Template techniques shown in Chapter 9 are invaluable in this situation.

Templates can also form the basis of zero-based budgets as, even when starting from scratch, an outline of the requirements for the budget is known and a template can form the basis of the new budget.

Summary

Budgeting is an essential part of modern management and is regularly performed in most organisations. It is as much a management philosophy and technique as an approach to financial accounting.

The spreadsheet is a particularly powerful tool in the development of budgets. It is also useful for the production of reports such as budget–actual–variance, year-to-date totals and consolidated results.

15

A Spreadsheet Budgeting System

It is a mistake to look too far ahead. Only one link in the chain of destiny can be handled at a time.

– Anonymous

Introduction

The budgetary control system described in this chapter illustrates how files can be linked in order to provide a flexible reporting facility. Figure 15.1 shows the modules of the system. The system is a quarterly plan for a single department or division and provides for the collection of quarterly budget figures and actual values. Options for producing variance reports and year-to-date reports are provided.

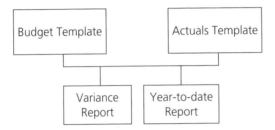

Figure 15.1 Proposed budgetary control system

Rather than develop a single, large file with the different modules on separate worksheets, separate files for each module will be created for this example. There are both advantages and disadvantages to linking data across files. One of the main advantages is that different parts of a system can be worked on simultaneously by different people. Probably the most significant disadvantage is that when there are many files to link the formulae can become very long and complex.

When embarking on a spreadsheet system that links cells across files it is advisable to keep the files in the same directory. The reason for this is that Excel keeps a track of the directory path when the links are established and problems can arise if files are moved, directory names or filenames are changed.

For the purposes of explaining how to develop a linked spreadsheet system for budgetary control, a small summary profit and loss account will be used as the basis for the budget. Obviously in a real situation the files will be larger, but the methodology is the same.

The system is supplied on the CD accompanying this book in a separate directory called BUDGET. The system then comprises three files called BUDGET, ACTUALS and VARIANCE.

Preparing the budget template

The summary profit and loss account is a deterministic model. Figure 15.2 shows the results of the plan after some data has been entered and Figure 15.3 is the data input form. This model has been designed using the template methodology described in Chapter 9 and has two sheets. The first is called *Budget* and contains the logic for the plan and the second is called *Input* and consists of the data input form. The file is saved with the name BUDGET. Although any name can be used it is important to carefully select the required

BUDGET.XLS

	A	B	C	D	E	F
1	Budget for 199X					
2						
3		Qtr1	Qtr2	Qtr3	Qtr4	Total
4	Sales	8000	8080	8161	8242	32483
5	Unit Price	37.50	37.69	37.88	38.07	
6	Revenue	300000	304515	309098	313750	1227363
7						
8	Direct Costs	6000	6090	6182	6275	24547
9						
10	Gross Profit	294000	298425	302916	307475	1202816
11						
12	Overheads	15000	15150	15302	15455	60906
13						
14	Net Profit	279000	283275	287614	292020	1141910

Figure 15.2 Budget plan with data

	A	B	C	D	E
1	Budget input form				
2					
3		Opening	Growth	Opening	
4		Value	Rate	Proportion	
5	Sales	8000	1.00%		
6	Unit Price	37.5	0.50%		
7					
8	Direct Costs			2.00%	of turnover
9	Overhead Costs	15000	1.00%		
10					

Figure 15.3 Data input form for budget plan

name, as the other files will reference it in the system. Once the budgetary control system is complete the four files can be saved as template files with an .XLT extension in order that they can be used repeatedly for different sets of data.

Once completed this file is saved with the name BUDGET.

Preparing the actual template

To minimise the work required for the actual file, open BUDGET, copy columns A and B to a new file, remove any existing data and shade the cells into which input is required. Figure 15.4 shows the first sheet of the actual file. As this is a quarterly plan, it has to be possible to enter four separate sets of actual data. Therefore the information in Figure 15.4 is copied into three further sheets and the sheets are named QTR1, QTR2, QTR3 and QTR4 respectively.

	A	B	C
1	Actual data for Quarter		1
2			
3			
4	Sales	8100	
5	Unit Price	37.50	
6	Revenue	303750	
7			
8	Direct Costs	130000	
9			
10	Gross Profit	173750	
11			
12	Overheads	12000	
13			
14	Net Profit	161750	
15			
16			
17			
18			
19			
20			
21			
22			
23			

Qtr1 / Qtr2 / Qtr3 / Qtr4 / Sheet6

ACTUAL.XLS

Figure 15.4 Template for Actual data with sample data for first quarter

To clarify which sheet is which, each sheet is also named as can be seen from Figure 15.4.

Once completed the actuals template is saved in the same directory as BUDGET with the name ACTUAL.

Preparing the variance report template

The variance report requires the user to select a quarter for which a report is required. The system will then select the appropriate range from the budget file and the actual file.

Figure 15.5 shows a variance report for the first quarter using the data for the first quarter's budget shown in Figure 15.1 and the actual data shown in Figure 15.4.

VARIANCE.XLS

	A	B	C	D
1	Variance report for Quarter			1
2				
3		Budget	Actual	Variance
4	Sales	8000	8100	-100
5	Unit Price	37.50	37.50	0.00
6	Revenue	300000	303750	-3750
7				
8	Direct Costs	6000	130000	-124000
9				
10	Gross Profit	294000	173750	120250
11				
12	Overheads	15000	12000	3000
13				
14	Net Profit	279000	161750	117250

Figure 15.5 Example variance report

The user enters the required quarter number in cell D1 and the following nested IF function is required in cell B4 to pick up the appropriate data.

In Excel:

```
=IF($D$1=1,[BUDGET.XLS]BUDGETS!B4,IF($D$1=2,[BUDGET.XLS]
    BUDGETS!C4,IF($D$1=3,[BUDGET.XLS]BUDGETS!D4,IF($D$1=4,
        [BUDGET.XLS]BUDGETS!E4,"!!!"))))
```

This formula can be copied to the remaining cells in the budget column of the variance report.

If a number other than 1, 2, 3 or 4 is entered, the above formula will return !!! in the cell. In addition the following IF function has been entered into cell E1:

=IF(OR(D1<1,D1>4),"ENTER A QUARTER NUMBER BETWEEN 1 AND 4","")

This will prompt the user if an invalid value is entered.

A formula similar to that used for the budgets is required for the actual column of the variance report, but with a reference to the appropriate sheet of the ACTUAL file. The formula in cell C4 is therefore:

=IF($D$1=1,[ACTUAL.XLS]QTR1!B4,IF($D$1=2,[ACTUAL.XLS]QTR2!B4,
    IF($D$1=3,[ACTUAL.XLS]QTR3!B4,IF($D$1=4,[ACTUAL.XLS]QTR4!
        B4,"!!!"))))

This formula can be copied for the remaining cells in column C. To complete the variance report the actual data is subtracted from the budget data. Therefore the formula for cell D4 is

=B4−C4

This formula can be copied into the remaining cells in column D.

Preparing the year-to-date report template

The variance report is designed to calculate the variance for any given quarter. However it is also useful to have a year-to-date report that shows the cumulative variance for a specified number of quarters.

Figure 15.6 shows a year-to-date variance report for two quarters.

This report works by adding together the budget and actual data for the number of quarters that are specified in cell E1. As the actual data is only added to the file when it becomes available, cell H1 reports the first quarter for which there is no data. Therefore with the above example it is only possible to prepare a year-to-date report for the first or second quarters as there is not yet any data available for the third quarter.

The following formula is required in cell H1 that will report the first quarter in which there is no actual data. If there is data in all

	A	B	C	D	E	F	G	H	I
1	Year-to-date report for how many quarters?				2		No data for quarter	3	Actuals
2									
3		Budget	Actual	Variance					
4	Sales	16080	16600	-520					
5	Average Unit Price	37.59	39.80	-2					
6	Revenue	604515	660750	-56235					
7									
8	Direct Costs	241806	210000	31806					
9									
10	Gross Profit	362709	450750	-88041					
11									
12	Overheads	30150	27000	3150					
13									
14	Net Profit	332559	423750	-91191					
15									

YTD.XLS

Figure 15.6 Year-to-date variance report for two quarters

four quarters, the cell will remain blank. This is achieved through the use of the "" at the end of the formula:

=IF([ACTUAL.XLS]QTR1!$B$4=0,1,IF([ACTUAL.XLS]QTR2!$B$4=0,2,
    IF([ACTUAL.XLS]QTR3!$B$4=0,3,IF([ACTUAL.XLS]
        QTR4!$B$4=0,4,""))))

The following formula is required in cell B4 to produce the year-to-date budget amount based on the number of quarters entered into cell E1.

=IF($E$1=1,[BUDGET.XLS]BUDGETS!B4,IF($E$1=2,SUM
    ([BUDGET.XLS]BUDGETS!B4:C4),IF($E$1=3,SUM([BUDGET.XLS]
        BUDGETS!B4:D4),IF($E$1=4,SUM([BUDGET.XLS]
            BUDGETS!B4:E4),"!!!"))))

If a number other than 1, 2, 3 or 4 is entered into cell E1, the above formula will return !!!, alerting the user to the fact that a valid quarter number has not been entered. This formula can be copied to the remaining cells in the budget column, with the exception of the unit price. It is not appropriate to accumulate a unit price and therefore the average unit price is calculated in cell B5 by dividing the revenue by the sales.

A formula similar to that used to calculate the year-to-date budgets is required for the actuals as shown below:

=IF($E$1>=$H$1,"NO DATA",IF($E$1=1,[ACTUAL.XLS]QTR1!B4,
    IF($E$1=2,SUM([ACTUAL.XLS]QTR1:QTR2!B4:B4),IF($E$1=3,
        SUM([ACTUAL.XLS]QTR1:QTR4!B4:B4),IF($E$1=4,
            SUM([ACTUAL.XLS]QTR1:QTR4!B4:B4),"!!!")))))

The first part of the above formula compares the number of quarters entered into cell E1 with cell H1 which is reporting the actuals quarter for which there is no data. If E1 is greater than or equal to H1, the message 'No data' is returned, otherwise the appropriate number of periods are accumulated.

As with the budget column, the formula can be copied to the remaining cells, but again the unit price is changed to be the average unit price by dividing the revenue by the sales.

The year-to-date variance is calculated in the same way as in the variance report by subtracting the year-to-date actuals from the year-to-date budgets. An enhancement is made to this formula to check the contents of actuals in order that the variance will be left blank if the 'No data' message is returned for the actual. Therefore the following formula is entered in cell D4 and copied for the remaining cells in the variance column.

=IF(C4="NO DATA","",B4−C4)

Summary

The four files that have been developed in this chapter describe a methodology for producing a flexible budgetary control system. The flexibility is primarily due to the use of separate files for each module of the system which means that different people can work on different parts of the system at the same time and users can choose to produce reports using selected data.

Before using the system it is important to ensure that all the files are in the same directory and that the links are correctly referencing the files. It might be necessary to select Edit Links and amend the path if the system is installed on another user's computer.

Consolidating Data

Man is still the most extraordinary computer of all.

– John F. Kennedy in a speech on 21 May 1963.

Introduction

The budgetary control system described in Chapter 15 is for a single division or department. In many organisations it is necessary to consolidate, summate or aggregate the data from separate divisions to produce a divisional or corporate report.

The consolidation options available in the spreadsheet allow for selected ranges of data from different files to be merged into a single file with options for summing, subtracting, averaging, etc.

To illustrate the consolidation features the variance report from the budgetary control system will be used.

Using the Consolidate command

Excel provides a powerful set of consolidation tools through the Data Consolidate command. However, before using the command a set of files to be consolidated need to be created. To do this open the *Variance* file and select a valid quarter number in order to produce a variance report. To simplify the consolidation procedure the range to be included in the consolidation is named by selecting the range A3:D14 followed by INSERT NAME DEFINE and call the range DATA_AREA.

To indicate that this is a variance report for a division enter *Division A* into cell A2 and then save the file as DIVA. To quickly produce another two files for this consolidation exercise change the division reference in cell B2 to *Division B* and save the file as DIVB and then change B2 once more to *Division C* and save the file as DIVC.

The next step is to create a new file that will form the consolidated report. Type an appropriate title for the report into cell A1 and then place the cursor on the cell that will be the top left cell of the con-solidated range, which for this example will be B3.

Select DATA CONSOLIDATE, which produces the dialogue box shown in Figure 16.1. The default function for the Consolidate command

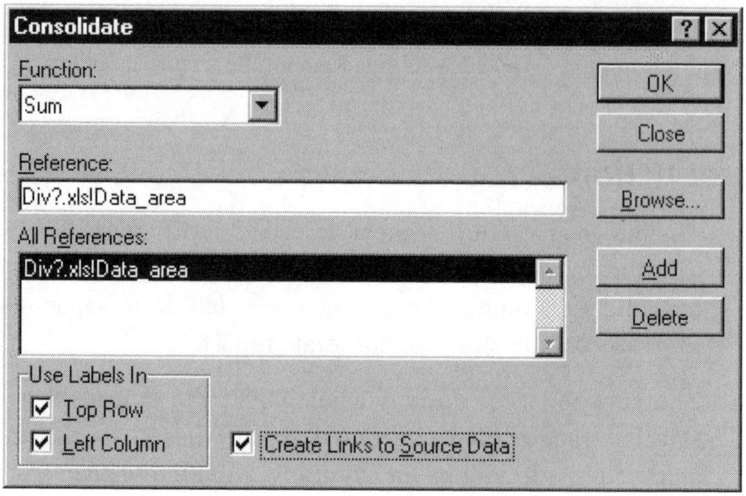

Figure 16.1 Data consolidate dialogue box

is SUM, i.e. the corresponding cells from the selected ranges will be summed. However, by clicking on the arrow to the right of the function box the other alternatives can be seen.

The reference box refers to the files or ranges that are to be consolidated. To complete this click on Browse and select the file DIVA. After the exclamation mark (!) type the range name Data_area and then change the *A* in *DivA* to a question mark (?). This is a wildcard that will replace any single character for the question mark. Click Add to put this reference in the list of references to be consolidated. The effect of this reference is that when the OK button is clicked the system will open each file beginning with DIV and take the range in those files called Data_area and sum them into the current worksheet. The range Data_area does not have to be in the same position in each file, but it should be the same size in each file in order that the correct cells are added together.

It is not always possible to name files and ranges with similar names and if this is the case each file and range to be consolidated must be individually selected and the *Add* box checked until the full list is displayed in the dialogue box. To illustrate this Figure 16.2 shows a completed dialogue box referencing the files separately with range references instead of the common range name.

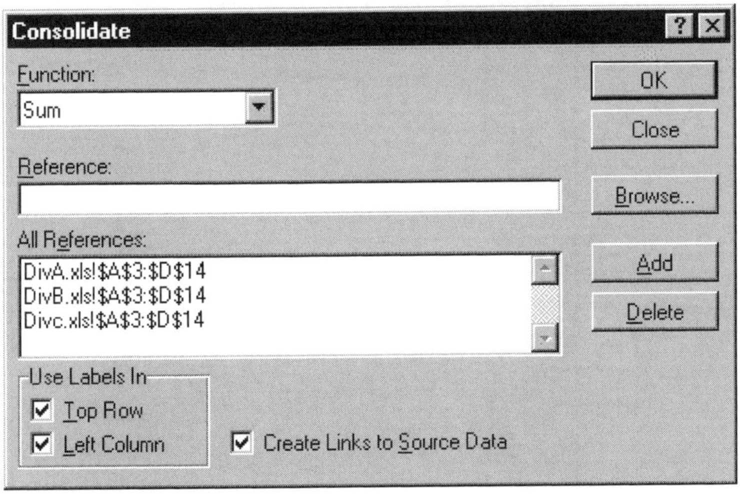

Figure 16.2 Consolidate dialogue box with separate references

Before clicking OK, check the three boxes at the bottom of the dialogue box to indicate that the top row and left column of the ranges to be consolidated are labels and that links are required to the source files. Figure 16.3 shows the results of the consolidation.

	A	B	C	D	E
1	Consolidated Variance Report				
2					
3			Budget	Actual	Variance
7	Sales		24240	25500	-1260
11	Unit Price		113.06	126.00	-12.94
15	Revenue		913545	1071000	-157455
19	Direct Costs		365418	240000	125418
23	Gross Profit		548127	831000	-282873
27	Overheads		45450	45000	450
31	Net Profit		502677	786000	-283323
32					

Figure 16.3 Results of Data Consolidate command

Because the *Create links to source data* box was checked in the dialogue box, the bar to the left of the report is automatically produced. By clicking on the number 2 the report is expanded as shown in Figure 16.4. This shows the data from all the ranges included in the Consolidate command.

	A	B	C	D	E
1	Consolidated Variance Report				
2					
3			Budget	Actual	Variance
4		Diva	8080	8500	-420
5		Divb	8080	8500	-420
6		Divc	8080	8500	-420
7	Sales		24240	25500	-1260
8		Diva	37.69	42.00	-4.31
9		Divb	37.69	42.00	-4.31
10		Divc	37.69	42.00	-4.31
11	Unit Price		113.06	126.00	-12.94
12		Diva	304515	357000	-52485
13		Divb	304515	357000	-52485
14		Divc	304515	357000	-52485
15	Revenue		913545	1071000	-157455
16		Diva	121806	80000	41806
17		Divb	121806	80000	41806
18		Divc	121806	80000	41806
19	Direct Costs		365418	240000	125418
20		Diva	182709	277000	-94291
21		Divb	182709	277000	-94291
22		Divc	182709	277000	-94291
23	Gross Profit		548127	831000	-282873
24		Diva	15150	15000	150

Figure 16.4 Expanded consolidated report

Looking at the data in Figure 16.3 the references to the three divisional files show the full path to those files and the totals contain a SUM function.

It is useful to be able to audit the source data of a consolidated report, but if a large number of files are being consolidated it may represent too much data. By not selecting the *Create links to source data* box, only the results will be produced in the consolidated report. This will result is a file much smaller in size, but it will not leave an audit trail back to the individual files.

Summary

The DATA CONSOLIDATE command provide a means of adding data together from different files without the need for linking files. This is especially useful when a large number of files need to be accessed as the file linking procedures require long formulae and take time to recalculate.

Index